THE STEEL CRICKET: VERSIONS 1958–1997

The Steel Cricket

VERSIONS 1958–1997

Stephen Berg

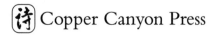 Copper Canyon Press

OTHER WORKS BY STEPHEN BERG

New & Selected Poems

Crow with No Mouth: Ikkyū

Oblivion

Bearing Weapons

The Queen's Triangle

Nothing in the Word

The Daughters

Clouded Sky by Miklós Radnóti (with Steven Polgar and S.J. Marks)

Grief

Oedipus the King (with Diskin Clay)

With Akhmatova at the Black Gates

Sea Ice

In It

First Song / Bankei: 1653

Homage to the Afterlife

Sleeping Woman (A public art collaboration, with painter Thomas Chimes, located on the Schuylkill River, Philadelphia)

TO WILLIAM KULIK

ACKNOWLEDGMENTS

"First Song/Bankei: 1653" was published by Harry Duncan at The Cummington Press, 1989, and also appeared in *Oblivion,* University of Illinois Press, 1995, along with "Daito's Mind," "The Not Two," the full text of "Sappho: You Burn Me," and "Lines/Vallejo."

Portions of "Sappho: You Burn Me" appeared in TriQuarterly.

The Machado, Blas de Otero, Hidalgo, Sabines, Greenberg, Stadler, and Annensky versions appeared in *Grief: Poems and Versions of Poems,* Viking, 1975.

"Down," "Infinity," and "Remembering Leopardi's Moon" appeared in *In It,* University of Illinois Press, 1986.

Nothing in the Word/Versions of Aztec Songs was published by Grossman/Viking, 1972, and was edited by Eric Sackheim.

"Altar of the Sun" by Octavio Paz appeared in TriQuarterly, 1958.

The book *Clouded Sky* by Miklós Radnóti was published by Harper & Row, 1972. The four "Postcards" that conclude *Clouded Sky* were published by Harry Duncan at The Cummington Press, 1970.

Sea Ice/Versions of Eskimo Songs was published by Harry Duncan at The Cummington Press, 1988.

Library of Congress Cataloging-in-Publication Data

Berg, Stephen.
   The steel cricket : versions / by Stephen Berg.
   p. cm.
   ISBN 1-55659-075-X (pbk.)
   1. Title.
   PS3552.E7S74 1997
   811'.54 – DC21   97-4653

COPPER CANYON PRESS • P.O. BOX 271, PORT TOWNSEND, WA 98368

Contents

4 | *Sea Ice / Eskimo Songs*

Preface

I have no idea exactly how or why Angèl Garibay's translations into Spanish of Nahuatl religious poems triggered the songs for *Nothing in the Word*. I know little Spanish, I tried to compensate for my ignorance with a dictionary. My impulse was a voice imagined, distilled from the much longer texts of the Garibay. I wrote in a kind of musical trance of prayer. A need of my own, a vaguely conscious "spiritual crisis" (Iris Murdoch in *Metaphysics as a Guide to Morals* calls it "metaphysical distress"), is a theme that runs throughout *The Steel Cricket,* and guided me.

Even before that, living in Mexico in 1959, struggling with my poor Spanish, I was amazed by Octavio Paz's ecstatic *Piedra de sol* and, using a bilingual dictionary as a crutch once more, found myself swept up in its vision of transfigured dailiness, its wave-like haunted chanting. Neither the Aztec Songs nor the Paz is wholly "accurate" in terms of literal sense, but both wish to be poems in English that echo enigmatic realms in both writer and reader.

Most of the versions in this book, however, are based on the English translations of scholars. I stumbled across them, they touched me, they offered fresh experience, unexpected imagery, strange logic. Often I heard a music that took over and led me to remake the texts.

One can argue that a poet's most ambitious love is the exercise of technical gifts, but I doubt it: he is pursuing something beyond poetry, for himself and the reader — a vision that embraces everyday life, a way of seeing, of thriving; insight that sparks a bit of understanding, the growth of the mind. That quest is likely to lead in almost any direction, no matter what the point of view or emotional context. When I was not writing my own poems, when silence was a witness against me, when by accident a text gripped me, I'd submit my "inner muteness," as Georg Groddeck calls it in his wonderful essay "Language,"[1] to other tongues, to a fusion of selves that I hope has resulted in durable poems.

Now, as I read through this book of nearly forty years, I think I see what that "beyond" may be — a yearning for sensations, hints, proofs, of some unity or force that would help me and the reader, to live "the mystery" with a deeper, clearer perception of what it is.

The mini-intros that accompanied some of the poems when they first appeared are glimpses of what caught me and caused me to write; they also sketch several of the various approaches I took. I include them here as the Appendix, with the exception of my Foreword to *Crow with No Mouth: Ikkyū*. Poems from that rather long portrait in free-verse couplets of a unique man's life in poetry are not included here.

Other omissions: in a recent volume of mine, *Oblivion,* a section of prose poems entitled "Rimbaud" very freely takes off from the Varése and other translations of *A Season in Hell.* Those texts belong together, as a single poem; a selection would have been inappropriate here. The same applies to the four main choruses in *Oedipus the King,* a project I wrestled with for three hard years with the generous, indispensable help of Diskin Clay and Bill Arrowsmith.

One book of mine, *With Akhmatova at the Black Gates* — its textual source also another English translation — fulfills a more original impulse and so falls outside the genre of "version" that defines this book.

A special case: Miklós Radnóti's *Clouded Sky*[2] is a book that was also translated collaboratively. Steven Polgar's native Hungarian, his gift for analyzing the poems as we worked together, were necessary inspirations that provided the foundation for the versions we all shaped.

A few years ago, my friend S. J. Marks died. It was his enthusiasm for Radnóti's poems that let us hear the heartbreaking voice beneath the rather awkwardly translated poems in an anthology of East European poetry. That first encounter with Radnóti's humbling, humane, tragic last poems is reported in a brief essay, included with the others in the Appendix.

In *The Steel Cricket,* my commitment to the everyday as opposed to my dream-fueled hunger for something more permanent, and my ambivalence toward that contradictory process, is what drove me. William Carlos Williams's reminder in his *Autobiography* that we are "inarticulate...like a litter of kittens in a woodpile" defines my search for ways to make sense of myself, of you, of *it,* if only for as long as a poem holds us.

Stephen Berg

---

[1]From *The Meaning of Illness,* Groddeck, International University Press, Inc., 1977.

[2]Out of print for many years, except briefly for the issue of *Poetry East,* edited by Richard Jones, that reprinted the book and sold out. *Clouded Sky* is one of this century's most important poetic records of political terrorism.

1 | *Bankei to Leopardi*

First Song | BANKEI: 1653

never was   always will be
mind before mind
earth water fire wind
sleep there tonight

you you on fire
burning yourself
attached
to this burning house

search
all the way back
to the womb
can't remember a thing

good bad
ideas
self self
which?

winter's wonderful
bonfire's
ridiculous
in summer

summer breezes
irritate
even before autumn's
over

rich now
you hate the poor
and forget when you
had nothing

you saved every dollar
a fiend
watched by the famished
wraiths of your self

your whole life
making money
could not pay off
death

clinging wanting
nothing on my mind
that's why I can say
it's all mine

you want someone you love
now
only because
you never knew her

you can't forget
not to remember
someone you never forgot
who?

looking back
you see it one brief evening
realize   see
everything's a lie

bitter? does this
incredible world of grief
hurt? why wound yourself
brooding on dreams?

no hands   no eyes
nothing exists
touch see
that's it

all this
is unreal
instead of clutching your head
go and sing

your mind
yours
torments you
because you need it

hating hell
loving heaven
torture yourself
in this joyous world

the hating mind
itself is not bad
not not hating
what's bad

good   bad
crumple into a ball
of trash
for the gutter

ideas about
what you should do
never existed
I   I   I

finished
with Buddhism
nothing's
new

enlightenment really?
"mine"
keep wrestling with yourself
idiot

these days enlightenment
means nothing to me
so I wake up
feeling fine

tired of praying
for salvation   look
at those poor beautiful flowers
withering

saunter
along the river
breathe
in   out

die   live
day and night here
listen   the world's
your hand

Buddhas
are pitiful
all dressed up   dazzled
by brocade robes

enemies
come from your mind
right wrong right wrong
never were

call it this   that
it doesn't exist
except this page
except these wavering phrases

praised abused
like a block of wood straight through
my head's the universe
can't hide my ugliness my clumsiness

so I just go along
with what is
without anger
without happiness

nothing to see   nothing to know
before after now
call and you'll hear
its heartbreaking silence

The Not Two | SENG TS'AN

the way is hard   choose choose
don't like or dislike   everything's clear
one hair between them   earth sky
not for not against   the truth is clear
for and against   mind's worst disease
no rest   deep meaning not understood
blank featureless space   just enough
taking rejecting   we think it isn't so
getting entangled   as if it's real
driving away pain   pretending it's unreal
pain vanishes   serene in the One
stop moving to rest   rest will be restless
linger on either   the One is lost
without the One   you're lost forever
get rid of Reality   sink deeper into the Real
clinging to the void   denies what it is
talk about it think about it   it's far away
not liking exhausts you   feuds do nothing
following the One   don't hate the senses
accept the senses   perception is true
the wise do least   folly shackles itself
why prefer anything   why be attached
why thought and thought   who led you there?
ignorance is rest unrest   no love no hate
dream ghost flower in the air   why try to hold it?
is isn't gain loss   bury them forever
eyes open in sleep   can't have bad dreams
not this or that   nothing but truth
the mysterious One   dissolves memories
think of the One   is is is is
no beginning anywhere   no battles left
movement is still   then where is it?
stillness moves   then where is it?

both gone forever   where is the One?
at the final point   with nothing beyond
no rules   all standards gone
all's equal   action is action
doubt's washed away   belief is easy
nothing left over   nothing remembered
don't speak don't think   everything's known
return to the root   the meaning's there
seek the light   you'll lose it's source
look into yourself   in a flash
what seems what is the nothing of it all   is yours
don't look for truth   give up your views
is isn't   breed chaos madness
the two exist because of the One   forget the One
no thought   no blame
no blame no truths   no nothing no thoughts
who does what he does   vanishes
nothing is done   when he's gone
who does what he does   does it
space is bright all by itself   no mind does it
no one understands   that amazing sphere
beyond yet here   neither he nor I
The Not Two   is the best form
nothing apart   everything here
this truth was   before all
forever and never   are the same
see it or not   it's everywhere
to trust in the heart   is The Not Two
The Not Two   to trust in the heart
and my serious words   mist
these things   that have no
yesterday   today   tomorrow

Daito's Mind

look
truth's naked radiant flesh
the core shines by itself
no eyes no ears

sky's like a sheet of pure aluminum

nothing
no words for it
desperate to find me
nothing you see

air's fragrant as an elephant fart

or here
is where I am
point to it
just like that

wet grass as tender as a baby's heart

without texts
you are it
just like that
try to see me

road's empty not a car man or dog on it

through form through sound
in either place
you can't see me
so many years begging

trees leafless like the bones of thought

robe's old torn
outside the gates miles of grass
sleeve tatter
chases the moon

hunched on my rainy stoop the old neighborhood cat
wandering everywhere
no footprints of mine are seen
on one tip of a hair I leave the capitol
three drum taps I leave Kyushu

car coughs two three times can't start

one glance at the morning star the snow got even whiter
the look in his eye chills hair and bones
if earth itself hadn't known this instant
old Shakyamuni would never have appeared

sink your teeth into this juicy arm

how boring to sit lazy on the floor
not meditating not breaking through
look! horses racing along the Kamo River
that's zazen!

falling asleep's waking to your first face

scoop up water
the moon lies in your hands
toy with a flower
its fragrance soaks your robe

one day I'll lift myself for the last time

please drink this cup of wine
beyond the Western outpost
you'll find
no friends

nothing but walls of mist miles ahead of you

full moon in the palace pond a gem
though it's not yet autumn
this noiseless night he's sure the ripples are different
from this alone he'll walk the path deluded

wrought-iron garden chairs like black skeletons

as if he had new eyes
huge Dantaloka Mountain hard as iron
cold windless night
but bamboo whispers

a world trying to know itself speaks in unison

I push away from the lamplight
the scroll of half-read texts
only my mind listening
not one master is left

this right-hand fist can't bang the sky's aluminum

mind slices a hair
blown against it nothing is cut it cuts itself
nowhere everywhere happens I hear
the emptiness gnash its teeth

taste its black mouth

Like That | BUDDHA

I came to crush time to study you to teach
Like a cloud drifting above you I darken everything I hide the sky
Crowned with lightning I save you with rain
Exactly like that like a raincloud I rise and point the way
Soothe your withered body know your pain ease it
Truth is the same for everyone — no hatred no love
Equal to all moral immoral I awaken all
When I rain down Truth you use it each in his way you live again
Shrubs grass bushes delicate plants huge trees
And the human world blossoms exactly like that
You I life death squeezed into a raindrop

I First Saw My Face | Yugi Jukichi

saw my face in a dream
first
one night of high fever
that wouldn't come down
crawled into bed slept
prayed to Christ
saw a face

not my everyday face
not my face as a boy
not one of those faces
you imagine —
yourself as an angel
that constant ideal face

the face was even better
and it was mine

some unacceptable blackness
tinged with gold
haloed the face

next day open-eyed
the fever was the same
raging high
but I was strangely calm

One Firefly | YOSA BUSON

for Clair

a dozing priest's white elbow night beginning

candle flame touches candle who holds it?

who'll use this little pillow twilight?

two huge doors of the gateway like shadows

yesterday faded and today and today

no underpants the wind blows back my robe cools my behind

sunshower look at the pimples on the frog's back sparkle

clunk of a bell struck carelessly muffled by fog

a woman raves and raves in a boat at noon though it's spring

someone's string broke yesterday his kite's still up there

not one bird warbles in the mountain's shadow

ploughing! the clouds did not move but they're gone

uguisu its tiny mouth wide open sings while the family eats

holding a butterfly by its wings just the feeling of it the
    mere feeling

a red plum's fallen petals flame on the horse dung

ghost shapes lean with the night toward dawn

shocked by my wrinkled hand plum blossoms what a
    ravishing smell!

in the cold corners of my room flowers glow

petals drunk on darkness on death

find out just how high the cherry blossoms are by standing there

rape-flowers a whale passes dims the sea

someone's thrown out a pot it yawns in the parsley patch

bone gatherer you know the violets better than anyone!

five-foot-high iris sticking up from a pond?

heartbreakingly puny beads of dew adorn the caterpillar's hairs

night's brief waves throb in an abandoned fire

scoop up that persimmon flower from a shallow well no stars

a wandering priest's coffin hauled past farmers plucking rice
        right now

oh the loneliness in the insane woman's face this summer

what scared the crazy chicken scrambling on my roof?

the path in such a downpour's invisible

it's terrifying this river with no name

sparrows clutching bushes gust after gust

gossiping rice farmers smash the moon against their knees

astonishing how the moon remains while nets and ropes are
        dipped and hauled up through it

a sandal in each hand he crosses the swift river

stonecutter's chisel dipped in clear water to cool

the priest's so happy hanging his mosquito net

one edge of it blows into my face

cool off kick my shadow fluttering in the stream

dawn fish that escaped the cormorants kiss the surface

even the woman who's divorced has to plant rice

sharp sickle chopping reeds fish hear it

a bat dashes by the wife across from my house glances at me

my fist in the darkness of my heart one firefly

one two three peony petals toppled on each other

clip the peony mind's empty

black ant so clear roams a white peony!

even after it dies the peony's image fills me

hawk shit splashed all across an iris

a priest can't decide whether to rip up the lotus

lightning wrecked that small house tangled in melon flowers

my feet at the bottom of the hot tub two strange white things!

it's a knife through me my dead wife's comb I stepped on in
          our bedroom

cricket crawls up the kettle hook freezing

more loneliness this year even more loneliness more

left my cane somewhere such sadness this evening

death soon plenty of time just to enjoy myself

an old friend out of nowhere stands in front of me

must have had a teacher but where where is he!

alone the moon's even more my friend

dropped my pipe in the lake studying the moon

white dew dampens hairs on the hunter's chest

murderer is the water deep where fog is?

fish strung up to dry from the eaves of a beach house get cold

lamplight through a crack in someone's door marks the
        village edge

a bottomless pail tumbles walks around in the storm

deer's cold horns pressed close to his body like withered twigs

deer cry out three times nothing now

dragonflies quiver on my beloved village's blue walls!

red maples suddenly black join the mountain shadow

young fox why did he cough on a hill of bush clover?

my indigo towel looks ugly beside morning glories

the candlewick's thinness all there is

melancholy crow in the bleak sky's the voice of human anguish

tiptoeing on dishes rats make a cold noise

ice creeps down edges of the well less and less

hate leaving my blankets to strike the snowy bell

a handsaw sounds like poverty this winter midnight

start the fire with that wooden Buddha!

shrewd birds scouring the onion patch what do you expect?

can't get rid of the love I feel this old man yearning again

snow on the stirrups of the waiting horse

snow snapping off twigs pierces the night and me

deep snow a priest pauses reading what's carved in stone

frost coats everything but a dandelion by my foot

bones grate against my quilt all night

the mountain stream's a solid path of ice

use my teeth to bite off ice from my writing brush

who left that red turnip on the riverbank in snow?

the high priest relieves his noble bowels in a desolate field

withered slope sunlight covers a rock instantly weakly

stars this early just before dark console the pale earth

the border guard's hibachi glows ice everywhere else

dog curled up against my door when he twitches rattles it dreams

oh to hide in myself sleep never be seen

the charcoal brazier warms the hem of my robe not my heart

the quilt down over my feet? up to my neck?

a roofer's footsteps squash leaves above my bedroom

twisting off plum branches sounds like my creaky elbow

Hat, Coat, Gloves | CÉSAR VALLEJO

The Regency Café's across from the Comédie Française and in it there's a secret room with an easy chair and a table when I go in the motionless dust has already risen between my rubber lips a cigarette stub smolders and two intense smokes are visible in the smoke oh the café's thorax and in the thorax a deep oxide of sadness it matters that autumn is grafted into autumns it matters that autumn is fused into young shoots the cloud into half-years the wrinkle into cheekbones it matters to smell like a lunatic postulating: Jesus, the snow is boiling! The turtle's so fast! How simple How is! How murderous When!

Lines | CÉSAR VALLEJO

Each ribbon of fire seeking love darts quivers in pitiful roses
      gives birth to the burial of the day before — I don't know
      if the drumroll where I look for it will be in clutching a
      rock or the endless birth of the heart

A grave plumb line stretches in hypersensitive axis towards the
      depth of beings — Destiny's thread! love will deflect that
      law of life towards the voice of man we'll be free in blue
      trans-substantiation we'll be virtuous against the blind
      and fatal

Within every pure zero isolated in fragile dawns may the
      superior Jesus from another great Beginning throb! And
      then one other theory — a Baptist who watches watches
      watches and rides an intangible curve with one foot bathed
      in purple

Poem Without Music | JOSÉ HIERRO

Wherever you are, you'll know what I'm saying, and why;
only you can interpret it,
can understand my message, which is very very simple:
purity, a bit of life, a little truth, are never forgotten —
although life, truth, purity, dissolve in our hands —
listen: these words are spoken only for you, only you will
      grasp them.
Some day, like this clear winter Tuesday in 1997 under pines,
you'll read these phrases, they'll resurrect a lost moment, deep as
      life itself,
and this will have done its work.
When that moment, which causes me to speak,
is smothered by custom, by a screen of superficial happiness,
you'll read this oblique record, and,
since what I say provides no facts, no information,
merely hints at what we both know without actually saying it,
you'll throw it aside, it will fall next to the skein of wool you are
      using up
to knit a coat for the son you will bear soon,
you'll laugh at the dreams and words that once stirred your soul.
I write as obliquely as I can so nobody penetrates the secret.
I use allusions because,
if you feel that moment has died,
nobody should hear its tune in his heart.
When you die, so has the poem.
When you forget, the poem will have ended,
like a single note scribbled in black ink on a calendar without days,
like a code you must break as long as the happiness I wanted,
      for you,
dreamed of for you,
has not dropped into your lap. And so,
you'll realize oblivion erases that moment.
If there is poetry beneath my words,

only you will know it.

It ends in you because you were its beginning.

Others cannot, should not, come close to its meaning.

That's all.

To Someone Who Loves Beauty | JOSÉ HIERRO

If you love beautiful words, don't stop here
to sniff these lines. How could you understand
these odorless, plain words? If you love clear water,
don't sip these red waters of mine,

and if you love looking up to follow the flight
of beauty, maybe you've never thought
how death prowls, how life and death, water and fire —
which have made pacts — are prying out, are loosening this rock

we stand on. As life grows perfect so does death, which we think
is far away. And everything else is
words, words, words,
those lovely, instructive things we — use.

If you love drinking wine from a silver cup,
you'll never find the path to the spring
that bubbles out of stone, you'll never lift
its pure liquid in your hands.

Life and death are your work. You weren't put here
to construct sea walls, to arrange things neatly
and spoil their miraculous chaos, you're here to name them,
to speak with them, not to contain their glory,

not to bring order, build houses;
you came to push the millwheel, to make it grind wheat
with your fleeting power. You are not here for you
("*My work,*" you say): life, death, that is your work,

a river spilling into the sea, "which is death,"
as those brave *coplas*, four centuries old, proclaim.
One day soon the songs you rewrote endlessly, and share,
the music of other waves will wipe out forever.

Defeat | RAFAEL CADENAS

I, who never learned how to do anything well
who felt weak faced with any competition
who passed up terrific opportunities
who arrived somewhere and immediately wanted to leave (because
        I believe moving on will solve things)
whom people abandoned and competent people humiliated by
        trying to help
who cling to walls in order not to fall down completely
who howl at myself
who believe my father was eternal
whom literature teachers humiliate
who was answered with chuckles once when I asked how I
        could serve
who will never build a home, be brilliant, be a winner
who have been left by many people because I rarely speak
who am ashamed for acts I haven't even done
who am often close to running off down the street
who have lost the center I never had
who am always jeered at because I live in limbo
who shall find nobody to put up with me
who was ignored so that others more wretched than myself
        could be considered
who shall continue like this and next year will be mocked
        endlessly for my ridiculous ambitions
who am tired of taking advice from lazier people
who shall never see India or anywhere because I cannot
who have accepted gifts and given nothing back
who wander from one end of the city to the other like a feather
        and let others carry me along
who have no personality and do not desire one
who stifle my defiant urges each minute
who have not joined the secret police
who have done nothing for my people

who belong to no freedom organization am desperate about all
 this and more — the list is endless —
who cannot escape my prison
who have been rejected everywhere because I am useless because,
 frankly, I've never really married or been to Paris or spent
 one peaceful day
who refuse to believe facts
who always drool over my story
who since birth have been an imbecile idiot moron asshole
who lost the thread of the speech I was trying to deliver to myself
 and have not found it
who do not cry when I need to cry
who am late for everything
who have been destroyed by too many advances retreats
who yearn for absolute immobility and immaculate punctuality
who am not what I am and not what I am not
who despite it all have fiendish pride although at times my
 humility has made me feel no taller than stones
who believe myself fated for something special and have
 achieved zero
who will never wear a tie
who cannot find my own body
who have glimpsed my deceit in heavenly flashes and haven't had
 the guts to throw myself onto the ground, to sweep
 everything away and start fresh and overcome my sloth, my
 drifting, my weirdness
who stubbornly go on committing suicide with whatever my
 hand touches
more absurd than I ever was, I, I am going to stand and mock
 myself more than ever and others too until judgement day

Bread | ANDRES ELOY BLANCO

"As good as bread…"
that's what they said to you,
wanting to eat you,
sitting at the table of their gestures,
wanting to taste your goodness.

I thought you smelled like a breakfast of love.
Your hands crumbled over the milk of your body,
your body grew brown with warm pity,
your heart whitened and became the heart of my bread.

That was the sacrament of your whiteness in my words,
your virtue in my ecstasy,
your imminent entry into my blood.
With a million hungers and thirsts my pores drank you.

I have sweated out my hates now
and my soul weighs no more than your bread in my hands —
girl as good as bread —
I wish I could take you
with the appetite of a child who has never sinned.

The Unknown Pain | LUIS PALÉS MATOS

I don't know exactly when but today
I started to think about that far-off pain
who knows where I'll be when it hits when it
breaks out from the inside   outside   or how
in rooms suburbs dreaming its bleak shadow
alive with prehistoric instinct

Sometimes from the hoarse shrill secret sea
from distances nobody has been to
inner   outer   echoes so indistinct
they lose themselves *talk talk talk*
like waves surrendering or is it praying
on the one motionless coast of mist and silence

Those voices those whatever-they-ares those
notes words are messages desperate letters
from ourselves from others we'll never meet
oh they try to prove with their despair   depth
those scenes inside we listen to fail
to listen to   screams of men overboard pleas
from a huge liner sinking in the distance

My God what limbos
swaddled in mist what unsuspected inner sights
everywhere we look some fresh horizon
pierces us   so deep so hard
we can't think can't understand
our lives grow in darkness

Maybe what happens inside us maybe
what feels tragic exists in those vague rooms
those mute outskirts of shadow   not one
pathetic shred of prayer reaches us   maybe

one night at a party laughing without a thought   you   I
are the backdrop against which such incredible pain…
no answer   its useless voice blows away

where am I
in solitude one solitude then another
in that strange unending timeless time of solitude

where is the light
do you have it
where
even the days are searching for you
the wounded days crucified
rise fall drip blood
the roads seek you
solitude upon solitude
my heart cracks in my chest

nothing returns
nothing is itself
everything's something else
nothing returns
nothing

flowers and grass
vanish
their fragrance barely reaches me
like a bell tolling hundreds of miles away
in another town
glances and voices
not yours
waters in other rivers
other leaves on other trees
everything's something else

nothing returns
the roads have gone
minutes and hours gone too
the river gone forever
like those comets we admire so much

my heart will spill out onto the earth
the entire universe will be my heart

Inscription | VICENTE HUIDOBRO

Stinking bird
no nightingale
sitting on my grave
fly up sing
listen to my hurt voice
I tried to make lovesongs
that would turn heaven into earth
I tried by suffering
well that was my own stupidity
now that I'm dead
now that I'm you
maybe God
will make me happy
I doubt it
but God can't wait
bird come back perch on my stone
weep make up a new song
the one I couldn't sing
leave one of your innocent tiny shits
on the silent marble

What Never Comes Back

| VICENTE HUIDOBRO

like a doorway without a door
you appeared
the hours changed
the night sky became dawn
the sea was a tree filled with leaves birds
flowers were happy
my heart gave off perfume

days walk through the year
where are you
my hands get longer
my gaze explodes
solitude weeps for company
silence is filled with your lost steps
I want other eyes to begin where mine end
where are you now
whose rooms do you warm
my heart swells like a sponge
like coral that joins to form islands

futile to look at the sky
futile to question the stones
each day grayer
futile to look at that tree
you are what distance is remoteness
and there's no cure

the days are looking for you
listen time sings like a nurse
while the wound sleeps

and my heart tries to escape
over the trees
and bursts against the sky

flowers
there they are
so what

Fatal | RUBÉN DARÍO

the tree feels almost nothing and is happy
the stone's happier feels nothing at all
this being alive this grief
consciousness
nothing's worse

where should we live terrified
of yesterday of tomorrow
of death which will come surely
when where
what do we know

touching your sweet body
reaching the grave
strewn with fresh branches
words driven back
by the silence

of endings
of our uselessness

Philosophy | RUBÉN DARÍO

Welcome the sun don't curse it live spider
Thank God you exist road out the window
Sweet vaginal mollusk crab fish bird
Be what you are: enigmas given form

Stop trying to fathom The One Law
Soon soon that duty will be God's
Chant bask in the fragile moonlight cricket
Bear waking to its kiss clap your big paws

Quatrain | ANTONIO MACHADO

God, you've torn out of me exactly what I need.
Listen to my heart thundering.
Your will be done, not mine.
God, now we are only my heart and the sea.

Poetics | MANUEL BANDEIRA

I've had enough
academic poetry —
public official phrases, polite lyrical verse
that punches a clock and tips its hat and says Thank You,
Mr. Director, Sir, Oh Thank You.

I've had enough poems
that stop and ponder the dictionary
to find out what's implied when a word's used in the vernacular.

Screw the purists — all words, especially barbaric universals, all
      constructions,
especially unique syntax, all rhythms, especially the ones you
      can count.

I've had enough lyricism dedicated to causes —
political,
rachitic,
syphilitic —
enough singing,
that worships
the outside world.

Anyhow, it's not lyrical,
it's what an accountant hears humming to himself
when he's doing your taxes, fantasizing all the ways
to seduce women, etc.

I want crazy drunk difficult pungent songs
like the ones Shakespeare's clowns recited
to bored kings,

I'm through with poems that can't make me free,
that go on and on bullshitting brilliantly
like a perfect lover who mouths all the standard lines —
etc. etc. etc. etc. etc.

I Don't See You | PEDRO SALINAS

I don't see you, but I know
you're nearby behind
a delicate cement and brick wall
close enough to my voice
to hear if I call.
But I won't call.
I'll find you tomorrow.
Blind to you,
I'll imagine
you always walk at my side:
the words I could not say yesterday
are enough for you,
tomorrow, when you stand
behind a delicate wall of wind,
skies, and years.

Inquest | MANUEL BLAS DE OTERO

I walk around everywhere, I have to find out what causes suffering,
the one reason for the suffering that's
bloody, tearful, but mostly dry,
cause of all the causes of the horrible things
done to men.
Not to Blas de Otero or Charlie, not Jeff, not to
Kulik or Berg, not Vallejo, no, that's not
what I mean. I go around looking
only for the cause, for the one cause
and the one suffering that's
always ready to begin.

What I'm asking is who gets pleasure from men suffering?
Who shaves for the sake of the pointless wind?
We know so little about what suffering is,
we're so proud of our pride,
but nobody can tell me anything about this when I ask.

Read the telephone book
or the Bible, it's easy to find something there.
I grab the telephone bible,
i hold on to
the Fisherman's Guide with both hands — and the dishes hit
    the floor.

Since age six
I've been hearing the same thing every hour — holy sky,
holy, holy — as if it issued from God at the end of His great work.

But when it comes to suffering, it's like the first day —
silences and welts of the double column. I can't stand it!

Enough | MANUEL BLAS DE OTERO

Imagine for a minute how miserable I felt
when I thought that God, the only living thing, doesn't exist,
or if He does is made of nothing except
earth, water, shadow, and wind,

and that death — Oh I'm shaking like crazy —
is an emptiness without even the light from a staircase,
a colossal hole that sinks endlessly
into a nothing of moist silence.

Then why live, sons
of mothers, at what windows be, crucified ones
and all you others? Enough death.

Enough. God, stop killing us wrong like this
or if you can't, just let us dangle way up
above you — howling river that overflows —.

Man | MANUEL BLAS DE OTERO

One body after another until death,
on the edge of nothingness, I cry out
to God, and his silence bounces back and chokes me.

God, if I have to die, at least
be awake. Night after night I still don't
know if my voice is going to be heard. I talk to myself.

I lift my hands, you cut off the fingertips.
I open my eyes to you, they catch fire.
I'm thirsty, salt flows out of the sand.

Here's what being a man is: his hands are full —
horrible! He exists, he doesn't exist — eternal, criminal
angel whose giant wings are chains.

A Clear Truth (fragment) | Manuel Blas de Otero

There's a moment like a strong man's cry of pain
between the abysses of being that gnaw on themselves
when God shows love and the body feels
His delicate hand touch us with an ounce of its weight.

Until then we have suffered so much silence,
we have looked everywhere like blind men so often,
we have been smeared with so much horror and emptiness,
that between all shadows His presence burns.

Grieve Like This | MANUEL BLAS DE OTERO

The little girls are multiplying in a high voice,
me for you, you for me, both
for the ones who still don't know how to do it soulfully,
the little girls sing in a high voice
to see if just once they can make God hear them.

Me for you, you for me, everybody
for peace on earth and a better country.
The little public-school girls throw a scream at the sky
but it seems the sky wants nothing from the poor.
I can't believe it! There must be a mistake
in the multiplying or the multiplier.

Those who have braids, may they be smooth,
those who wear frilly underpants, may they fall down immediately,
and those who don't have anything but a tiny snail
may they unwind it in the sun,
and together at the same time recite in a high voice
me for you, you for me, both
for all those who suffer on earth, crushing
the one who counts.

No | JOSÉ HIDALGO

The night smothers you so I look for you
like a maniac in shadow, in a dream, in death.
My heart burns up like a single bird.
Your absence murders me, life has closed.

What loneliness, what darkness, what a parched moon slips by,
what distant people are looking for your lost body.
They ask your blood, your lips, your sound,
your inseparable absence in the growing night.

My hands don't hold you and my eyes miss you.
My words look for you on foot, uselessly.
Inside me the quiet night is long, lies down,
stretches like a river whose banks are lonely.

But I go on looking for you, digging you up, dissolving you
in shadow, in a dream. I nail you down in memory.
Silence creates your unsayable truth.
The world has closed. For me, permanently.

Monday Passes | JAIME SABINES

Nobody can live faced with truth
and not grow sick or depressed in the middle of his bones
because the truth is we are weak and miserable
and need to love, hope, believe, and say *Yes*
like a tree opening.
What a beautiful word "God" is — long
and useful against fears.
But Monday passes like a big yawn, Tuesday, Wednesday, all the rest,
all of them, and life passes like these words
between getting drunk and asking forgiveness,
between empty hands and empty heart,
with memory like a window carved out of darkness.
I say this because someday I'm going to open my eyes
and see your eyes, open forever
like the word "God."

Saint Francis

We will take the road
God wants us to take

hold to the thoughts
you are thinking now
they are good and helpful to you
inspired by God

my dear companions
pray
to possess the infinite treasure
of holy poverty

don't rush away
I will arrange
what you should do
for the salvation of your souls

small is the suffering of this life
but the glory of the new life is infinite

2

Saint Francis believed in the invisible
and spoke to birds
we do not believe in the invisible
we do not speak to birds

3

My little bird sisters
praise Him because he gave you
freedom to fly anywhere

gave you
double and triple covering
brilliant pretty clothing
food ready for you
singing
the domain of the air
springs to drink from
high mountains hills rocks crags for shelter
tall trees to rest in

therefore my little sisters
be grateful always
strive always to praise God
He loves you very much

First Twilight | ARTHUR RIMBAUD

Huge indiscreet cunning trees
clawed the windowpanes,
pressed close —
she wore almost nothing

perched in my fat armchair,
hands folded on her petticoat.
Exquisite feet
quivered on the floor,

one wand of waxy light
crisscrossed
ecstatic lips, a fly
droned on a rosebud nipple,

a circle of faint clear trills
like a shocked crystal chandelier
broke from her mouth
when I licked her ankles

and both my hands
chased wild feet
through layers of white lace — "No!"
she giggled, clenching her thighs.

Oh those bleak animal eyes —
I grazed each lid
with wet lips.
"Too much!" Her head shot back.

"I want to tell you…"
I completed her sentence with my tongue

which made her laugh again,
mercifully this time, ready...

Huge indiscreet cunning trees
clawed the windowpanes,
pressed close —
she wore almost nothing.

Defilements | ARTHUR RIMBAUD

ancient animals fucked running
glans filmed with excremental blood
our fathers showed their cocks
unsheathed them pulling the scrotum out to display it
you needed a huge one to fuck women or pigs
don't envy a rhino's we're big enough

but sadly we've given up wielding our shlongs in public
showing off like children frolicking in the woods
often I've watched men
shitting behind hedges
learned what the ass is for
white screened by hair

women have a tuft of it right there
focused like a dark flame
anything to be naked studying it
I also dreamt of eating the deep pink lips that pout
after fucking wet with my sperm
dreamt my mouth was often
open on it
as if proof of a soul depended on that act
as if that were my soul
kneeling sucking on it weeping

My Little Lovers | ARTHUR RIMBAUD

Something like human tears
soak the cabbage-leaf sky,
trees drool,
your raincoats laid out
white with unique moons
like big round eyes
beneath branches.
Hideous children,
slam your kneecaps together
until they ache.
Blue ugly one,
we were in love then,
we gobbled soft-boiled eggs
and chickweed! Blond ugly one,
one night you gave me the holy name of "poet."
Drape yourself on my lap
so I can lift your skirt and whip you.
Black ugly one,
redheaded ugly one —
I vomited your brilliantine.
O my petit amours,
I hate you,
I'd love to see your tits plastered
with blisters, all my sentiments
smashed like mossy old flowerpots.
Jump up, dance for me,
a star pinned to your limping backs,
flex those gaunt shoulder blades
that inspired me to rhyme.
I'll break your hips
for loving me, for getting me hard.
Sweet ugly ones, vile ugly ones,

stale mound of stars, failed, fallen
through the abyss of God's absence,
my dried saliva glistens on your brow.

Memories of a Simple-Minded Old Man

| ARTHUR RIMBAUD

If there's a God, forgive me!

As a boy, at country fairs, I avoided
the idotic shooting gallery's metal ducks, pushovers,
clones gliding across cartoon water under a cartoon sky;
I stood awestruck in the screaming crowd
where worn-out donkeys went at it
with that long bloody tube, which still stuns me.

Oh, and my mother! —

her nightgown smelled like vinegar,
hem frayed, yellow as a lemon.
My mother! She'd climb into bed
appallingly, making such noise,
my mother with her full rich thighs
whose ripe buttocks pinched the linen sheet between them
and drove me wild — should I be saying this?

A cruder calmer shame:
my sister, home from school, peeling her ice-wet bloomers down
so I could watch a delicate thread of urine
squirt from her tight pink lips!

Forgive me!

Sometimes I saw my father, evenings, cursing,
playing cards with his neighbor — me they pushed away —
    things seen...
a father's scary...kids imagine things!
His knee, rubbing against a leg at the table,

his pants, his fly I wanted to unbutton — stop me! —
to hold the thick dark cock of this man
whose hairy hand rocked me!

And I won't talk about
the pot, the omelette pan, the handle, glimpsed in the attic,
almanacs streaked with blood, basket of lint,
the Bible, the maid fingering herself,
The Holy Virgin and the crucifix.

Oh, no one
was aroused so often, no one was so amazed!
Dear Lord, forgive me,
bathe me in Your grace, hear my confession,

let me speak to You as I would to a friend.
Puberty's never left me, and it grows, and the disgrace
of my tenaciously sensitive penis! Why,
why the dark so slow at the base of my belly, why
infinite terrors constantly burying my joy like black gravel
scattered by an anonymous hand?
That I exist astonishes me! What can I know?

Forgiven? O childhood! Nothing has changed.
I reach down: Lord, let's both of us jack off!

Flutes in the Sacred City | SIMONIDES

When hard times hit, a man's bad; when good times come, he's good. The best men are the ones the gods love. So I'll never expect to find one man who hasn't sinned or isn't crippled — if I find him anywhere on earth I'll let you know. I'm for the man who doesn't ruin his life, who doesn't fight against necessity. That's how the gods live. But I'm not looking for faults. It's enough for me if a man isn't too good or too bad and knows what's right for the perpetuation of cities. He's a sound man, I won't blame him. The worthless go on and on and on; things go well when nothing vile creeps in.

If you're mortal, don't talk about tomorrow. If you see someone who's happy, don't even think about how long he'll be...change goes anyway it wants to, faster than the dragonfly left right up down suddenly.

Even the oldest men who were called half-gods didn't get there without toil, the malice of others, danger.

Oh everything gets trapped between two huge rocks that grind against each other — poems, love, children, friends, everything, even money.

Man is weak and things worry him and it doesn't stop. It's one labor after another in a short life and whatever he does death hangs over him and can't be escaped. Good men and bad men share it equally.

The only man who deserves praise would pit the force of a gravestone against rivers and flowers and the heat of the sun and the full golden moon and against the waves of the ocean, breaking, breaking. The gods control all these but a stone, or human hands, can break them. Ridiculous!

Who are you? You'll be the opposite. What do you have? You'll get the opposite.

Everything sinks into the ground, even your talent.

The dust from wheels sprays up on both sides like wings lifted by a gust of wind.

So many birds nobody could count them circled his head, fish jumped right out of the water when he sang, when he let out his incredible song, broke completely free of the blue water.

Nothing moved, nothing except the heaviest leaves quivered a little, and someone's beautiful voice struck people's ears.

Bees tread the flowers and stay there and drink until the honey starts.

They say virtue lives on a high perilous rock, hard to climb, surrounded by a troop of pure innocent girls, and you can't see her, virtue, unless you eat your heart out and sweat blood and reach to the very peak of being a man.

Silence is so valuable it's no risk.

What's worth doing unless there's pleasure in it? — not life itself or a throne. Not even a god wants to go on living without pleasure's succulent dark cunt on him.

Nightingales, green-necked birds that appear in spring...blue swallow, carrying the vast sweet breath of spring...

Even how things *seem* roots out the truth.

The sky has the sun, nothing else; a breeze wrinkles the sea.

The cock's voice is amazing...wind breaks the sea into two gates...bringing man to his knees...an arrow with three barbs on it ...like music gliding any way it can, like the hound following the deer until it clamps her neck in his teeth and bites hard and thrashes it any way it can...I know how to sing to the bride, to dance with light feet!

Only a god feels no guilt and does everything.

The city teaches the man.

The citizens of Corinth immortalized what they did by honoring the sky's gold; that gold increases and spreads their fame and their father's fame; when the sky shines it's the kindest host there is, but it's an ugly guest when people fill their hands with it.

Luck helps the brave.

But Homer, the man of Chios, said this, and it wipes out everything else —"A man's life is like the life of a green leaf"— so few men who hear it fold it in their hearts, because we all feel hope, especially the young, and as long as there's a fleck of smooth skin anywhere on a man he believes nothing can end and nothing ages and death doesn't exist and he doesn't even think about sickness. What poor fools we are. Why don't we face how short life is? Listen to me — think of time, and when you approach the end, give yourself easily, freely, gratefully.

Ten thousand years are as brief as the sun flashing off a grain of sand nobody will ever see.

Don't touch some things or fight with men who are deeply attached to their gods.

God and only God cures sicknesses.

Not even a single grape pit should be thrown away because wine makes us feel wonderful!

Two handles on one cup so we can both hold it and drink!

I lie beneath stone, yes, but the incredible strength of the lion shakes this stone, just as the man I guard shakes the earth with his power. How could a lion have been called *Lion* without a spirit that could still wander like this?

Somebody's glad I'm dead and somebody will be glad when he is. We're all debts owed to death.

I stumbled across this corpse on an island one day when I was out walking — O God, kill anyone who kills me the way you killed this man, but make those who bury me happy.

What about the women who prayed their men would be filled with a love of war?

War and freedom! Since the sea first split apart and made Europe and Asia and the insane war god haunted the cities of mankind, men haven't done anything greater — first they hacked down our countless enemies on shore, then they took hundreds of ships and the men on them, and Asia screamed when both hands closed around her neck.

This bow, these arrows that sleep under the roof of Athena's temple, their sad job done, often in the worst battles drenched themselves in the blood of the murderous Persian horsemen.

Lean forever, muscular fine long shaft of ash, against this tall pillar, you'll always be sacred. Your fierce bronze head is old now, you've grown haggard with so much handling in war.

Everything, even the strongest man, is crushed and blown away by time's butchering teeth and all work is measured by time, which can strip open a man's chest and show us his heart.

We died here, protecting Greece, thousands and thousands of us, fought arrows, horses, and men. Oh stranger, we have famous names and unknown names and everybody's name, we saved Greece with our own lives when her fate dangled by a hair, we wrapped death's black misty cloak around us. Glory keeps us alive because we strove for freedom. The mad war god plunged his spear into the bloody lake of our breasts and instead of spearmen this dust covers whatever dead bodies are called. One sea, one night, one ship, one soil, one people.

Child of the dark earth, grasshopper, these flutes playing in the sacred city play for you.

from The Trojan Women | EURIPIDES

HECUBA: What are gods?
When I look at my life, I know what they are:
masters of pain, forces that made my life hell.
And out of all the world's cities they chose Troy to hate.
We made sacrifices. What did they mean? Nothing.
But what if God's hand — think: His hand! — what if
    that hand
hadn't reached down and crushed Troy and smeared it
    into the ground
like a smudge of ash? Then piece by piece Time
would have swallowed us until we were nothing,
we'd be air, we would never have lived, as we do now —
the grief-stricken immortal theme of so much
    human music,
of so many songs men will sing — forever.

Oh lay Astyanax in his poor tomb, go now.
Those frail, traditional flowers, white as the white of a
    baby's eye,
are his. Let them shrivel on his breast, below.
What difference does it make to the dead
if they pass into earth accompanied by gold and silver,
by any luxury they enjoyed in life?
Those are the hollow objects of desire
in which the living love their own beautiful faces.

Down | ARCHILOCHUS

Wait. Listen. Don't move.
There's a girl working in your house
who's so beautiful, so alive
anyone would want her.
We should sit down
some night over wine and I'll tell you
how often I've seen in my mind
the tight silky hair of her cunt
glistening beneath the moon
and wanted to ease my tongue in.
Remember that great saying —
Love gives men things other than the pure face of God
        to enjoy —?
I confess
once, months ago,
I took her into the fields — it was spring: shaggy
tall red flowers bobbed in the grass everywhere.
I helped her down and slid my hands under her neck
and pillowed her with my wool cloak.
She sat up for a second, afraid,
but I kissed her nipples gently, with such tenderness
how could I stop myself
from dropping between her thighs.
She quieted and let me touch her everywhere,
her firm skin shone, sweating with lust,
I licked her throat, armpits, feet, navel, knees,
and in her for the first time came
the moment my wild cock
sank halfway in —
to her thick, blond, flowery bush.

In the Spear | ARCHILOCHUS

I love politics but I can sing
as variously as a bird's wing

just as my short-cut hair
makes me dangerous in war

no bows no slings a bare sword
close to my enemy's face

in the spear my dark bread
in the spear Ismarian wine

I drink leaning on my spear
walk with me cup in hand

along the benches of the ship
dip from the hollow tuns

drain the red wine's dregs
drunk on this watch as any would be

though I dropped my shield
poor blameless instrument

next to a bush and some Saian uses it
at least I saved myself

who gives a shit for a shield
I'll get one just as good

Oh little will be left of my life
a phrase a poem pieces of my voice

I never cared what men thought
that way I enjoyed myself

whatever I did I didn't whine
about bad luck I ate and drank

no matter how many friends drowned
the gods taught me to survive

the gods taught me we die
one man today another tomorrow

and most men stay friends
as long as they can use each other

what men do is toil & fear
fate luck give a man all he has

my island of exile Thasos
like the backbone of an ass

a savage wood at its height
the banks of Siris I love far away

when my sister's husband died at sea
I refused to write or sing

but tears won't heal anything
dances won't make it worse

fuck money fuck the gold of golden Gyges
their lives in the arms of the waves

I don't envy the gods' power
who wants to be a king

I'm some kind of unknown master of
I really don't know or care

Apollo kill the guilty
appear speak to me

I can see again one girl's ravishing face
her hands hold myrtle and rose tree

I can see her long dark hair
veil her shoulders and back

so fragrant even this old man
is stirred to the core

drink to the tune of the flute
drink the Phrygian ale

talk like an old lecher
to yourself in your dying head

like a shadow thrown on a wall
desperate to keep it all

many things cheer a man's heart
hair cut short for battle

meat on a long table
like the proud ox I own

who knows his work and won't budge
on the cliff between sea and wind

that's where I live
waiting for an omen

a good man a skilled steersman
while thieves stalk the city

while thousands of years after me
a stranger plunders my voice

idle simple-minded dumb
his crude words try to find me

in the dust of texts
O desolate citizens

understand what I say
don't yearn for Paros and the life of the sea

look the immense waves the clouds
announce a storm death's always near

only the gods know what victory means
trust everything to the gods

often they raise to their feet
those laid low on the black earth

often they crush fortunate men
who seemed so strong

and starve and drive men insane
I don't love tall generals

nor the half-shaven man proud of his hair
a man should be bowlegged short

planted on the ground full of heart
no man gets glory when he's dead

let the living help the living
the dead are like any shit

say nothing against the dead
but one great thing I know

how to stick evil up the ass
of a man who's done it to me

soul my soul confused by hopeless troubles
look up fight off ambushes

don't rejoice if you win
don't grieve if you lose

knowing how men are
how friends can make you choke

I'd love to wrestle you
as much as I love to drink

but nothing surprises me
nothing's impossible now

that Zeus has blocked out the sun
a terrifying black disc at noon

from now on believe nothing expect nothing
let nothing astonish you

even if horses graze on the sea
and dolphins crop grass

and the loud sea itself by a farmer who loves hills
is loved more than those hills

me chanting starting with my flute
Lesbian songs Archilochus who knows

his mind stormy with wine
how to lead off Dionysian revelry

smashed on unmixed wine
shameless I'll say anything

my voice less and less mine
my songs shattered by the years

desire loosens my limbs
desire overwhelms

like this curse I hurl watching you
on that high rock over there

as time rips me apart as time eats my words
and some fake scholar unearths the shards

of my heart and patches them together
like this curse on an old friend

chain him sicken him let him freeze
stretched on his belly like a dog

swallowing seawater helpless
on the edge of the surf

vomiting his meal of waves
who broke his promise

but under it all the cure
to be pierced by song

faced with death as you see
your own skin withering

though love's fire twisted itself
like a snake beneath your heart

and bit thick mist across your eyes
and stole your gift of thought

Zeus alone can predict
what will happen to you

and no force exists to put back together
what you did who you were

your soul your voice other men's quotes
echoes of someone else

yes yes the poppy's green
revenge may find you

whatever glimpse of a man makes sense
or makes no sense

as long as you still hear
shadows of his mind echo

luck highest of all shined on us
each of my spears hit home

always war war always fixed inside me
somewhere waiting to find me

that's why I drink like the gods fearlessly
that's how I kill so many

that's how I wed my beautiful whore
one thousand men before me

javelins shields in my brain I hear
stones shift in the wall lyre-players

axes bows hair shaved from a shield-handle
the enemy crushed humbled waiting for dawn

like the scattered clamor
of a skeleton's moan

I was a spark of fire
I was a dim reef

I was a human hand
afflicted with lice

I was an eeryl or cock-halcyon
whose beak was green

I lopped off one soldier's genitals
I lifted a cricket by the wing

I unyoked myself
a slave overweening

one mind and it blazed fully white
the weapon of my skill meant suffering

curly-haired idiot silly fig-nibbler
raving I gobble barley-cakes

chewing the morsels
savoring each tiny grain

with an ape's ass
and foam blossoming on my mouth

yes yes the poppy's green
despair's furious nonsense

O singer we all must call to if we are to sing
say somehow to my listeners

my shield can't be found anyplace
not one dear friend is left to walk with

from "Sappho: You Burn Me"

you burn me   burn me burn me

these arms can't touch the sky

whose   his   yours   do you love him

two minds   better

to me

wind   heart of a little child

fantasy

there is   the problem of the night

touch   O who   and I yearn for you

who cannot touch the sky   well one day I saw

the prettiest girl
picking flowers

there is   the problem   of

of dawn

sleep next to me   fingertips graze my face

the bright and beautiful belong

what a thought   to the desire of the sunlight

nothing destroys

gold   moth worm   nothing can eat it

not one human heart has ever resisted it
or the moon

>

this gold cup with knobs like knucklebones halfway down

O moon moon   time
never stops   I'm alone

I could say what I remember about you is

purple handkerchief   gift   giver

a wildness crushing
ingenuous

>

I prayed our night would be two nights

moonlight filtering through your gown   two
radiant nipples   and the dark sweet
triangle

>

honey   bees   none
and death
with or without love

>

the Gods hate death
if not they would die

>

and I'm already dead

or why would I   is this the deep shame often
why would I   my love's   insatiable
          haunted by terror

                              ➤

there is
                              this
seeing I see things   gods passions

          my arms   legs   my whole body
     stars flung on the sky

                              ➤

     because forever nobody will ever
          touch me   dust
oh touch me now   kiss these eyelids breasts thighs

                              weeds
the moon   right there above your shoulder

                              ➤

                              stars in an
     unknown order   could it be this voice trying to return

          my heart and your heart touch
          I can feel how we
          will always shine back
          fair face upon fair face

          deeper than flesh and blood

                              ➤

Brocheo
sitting watching your face   I can barely breathe
what are you   I a god like this   given your voice
given your soft laughter
I can barely speak

Brocheo who are you
veiled eyes there's a singing trembling sweat trickles from every pore
nothing's left I'm pale green grass to my soul   poor

delicate fire and death and a dark burning
time again   time   threshold as always

O mind
dream   and in it a sign   Hermes   I told Hermes

I wanted to die

>

sapling
standing in the bright air   marry her

>

love has shaken me

like wind rushing down from the hills
hitting a grove

of oaks
you burn me
with what eyes look me in the face
friend to friend

nothing's sweeter than sleeping with your love
      it heals the dying soul

with what eyes
          what pain love gives
you burn me   show me   what's behind your

                eyes

        a breeze now   what is

Infinity | GIACOMO LEOPARDI

That hill out there — I've always loved it! —
and this hedge, cutting in front of me,
blocking the horizon, the last step to infinity.
Sitting here, stunned by a dream of space
beyond all hills and hedges, I hear
silence erasing man's possibilities.
A calm starts inside me and stays for a while.
Wind roughing the trees, weighed against silence, is eternity.
This is the season of the mind —
the dizzying gulf of sky, the abyss of self —
one distant, visible; one close as my own skin —
each impossible to know or to touch,
this is the time when consciousness and thought and I
are nameless, nothing, not here. I love it —
the one true freedom: letting my mind sink
like a ship in midocean whose keel
is smashed by some invisible
fist and goes down with the sweet ease of a rock.

Remembering Leopardi's Moon

after GIACOMO LEOPARDI

Moon, the year is over.
I scaled this hill a year ago to see you.
My heart was rapid and cold, you
floated over the maples, there,
the same pasty communion wafer you are now,
you made each leaf visible,
you made the road leaving this fortress glow like an eerie snake.
But I could barely see.
In a dream, on one of those nights
when I know I'll die, the whole world
looked crippled, poor, free, everyone stood outside
pointing at you, whispering.
Moon, if I love anyone, it is you.
And then I love a girl fondling me, and games, and my body
when it was straight, gray-veined, milky,
before my father's violence turned it ugly.
It feels good to look back,
to count how many years I've lived,
to resurrect images of childhood. Time,
death, love, quivered with hope then.
I'd climb trees and let myself slip from the top,
trusting the branches to break my fall.
You'd be there, guarding me.
But I feared violent noises and the dark.
At ten, my life was over.
I'd sit in my father's stone library
and read, read with my brother Carlo
in an alcove, drop off to sleep in his lap,
reading. I was healthy until I was ten.
From ten to seventeen I sat in that jail and read —
my father forced me —

until I became those pages: yellow, infinite.
But I won't waste time now trying to see again
what was. Pain's made the world abstract.
Clouds, stars, the night: that's all. Moon,
where are you? Look at me: a hunchback
dressed like a stupid, vicious priest. Pure black.
I pit language against despair each minute of each day
to breathe, to act, not to feel crazy —
the only way I can touch you.

Nothing exists, not even this voice of mine,
these simple words. Illusions are gone:
desire, hope, those two
that made waking possible, dawn after dawn.
They used to make me tremble,
but nothing has value, earth does not care,
life is the narrowness of this poem,
the grind of composition, and what I write —
truculent, useless (though it begs to live) —
is dust even before it reaches your ears.
Sleep. Go back to the chaos of beginnings. Stay there.

No moon above those cool, featureless trees: black
emptiness, which is time, which is —
if we can bear it — all the world is.
The mute path of the stars is crazed, magnificent.
The breeze just now freshens my heavy face.

Nature, sickness, people struggling to love —
what do they mean? Time is the breath of gods,
the air of cities and rich fields,
it gorges each thought, cell, blood and bone,
it is the gods, it is our consciousness,

it means we now
are,
we are,
you, I,
(oh why isn't a hand rubbing my twisted spine?)
are,
each word next to a word stone.

from Purgatorio, XVIII | DANTE ALIGHIERI

Oh how the mind loves immediately whatever pleases it
and acts to get what it wants
your gift of touch smell sight
etches an image of the world inside your flesh
and the mind turns to it feels love
(to turn like that is love)
repeats itself for pleasure then like fire
whose shuddering tongues stab upward
from stuff that makes its wild shapes possible
the captive mind inhabits desire
whose every move is spiritual
and can't rest until
what it loves makes it rejoice
I hope you know that those who say each love is wonderful
are far from the truth
not everything that stamps the wax is good
though the wax is

2 | *Nothing in the Word*

AZTEC SONGS

which flower
should I believe in
born here
O first one
which gift
in the place where both sides are

with ropes of flowers
our flowers are braided together
beautiful is your word
you breathe it here O first one

open your heart like the flowers
I want to live near your heart
you hate me you prepare my death
now I am going to your house
you should cry for my tears
you should own my sadness
Oh my friend but
I am going I am going to your house

so many wings come here
dipping honey
and speak here
in your house Oh
god

it is so hard
to live like this!
no happiness on the earth
for me

we live on earth
lent
here we are
men
over there ones without bodies
in your house
here home between
a little while only

only with our flowers can we find pleasure
only with our songs does our sadness dissolve

until today my heart was happy
I hear this song I see a flower
if only they would never wither
EARTH!

in god's house
I was born for nothing
for nothing I am leaving the earth
BROKEN!

a little time at your side
Oh you through whom all of us live
truly
you carve the destiny of a man
can you touch me feel me
here on earth

black flowers wrinkled with gold
fill the beautiful song
the singer sings with the veins of the eagle
with many flowers torn from man

do you exist do you really exist
sometimes I have gone looking for you
Oh for whom do you live
do you exist do you really exist
this is what we say
don't break our hearts again

I begin to sing
I lift high
the song for you
through whom everyone lives

now you revive us
how have you done it
with your roots
I decorate myself
I will fly
I am miserable
from this weeping

on the edge of war near the bonfire
we taste knowledge

because I cry
because I am desperate
I am left alone
there is no compassion on earth
how can I live among men
even at your side
god
I am bitter

we disappear
eagles tigers
nothing in the gold
nothing in the emeralds
nothing in the feathers
nothing in the word

over there now
it revolves throbbing
the bee
here gold flowers open
there you are O first one

I am going to guard the mountain
in a place of sadness
you breathe
you cry
I bring together my god songs
I breathe
I cry

this is the place
where life is given
O first one
with these flowers
dance here
in the middle of the flowers

where are we going Oh where are we going
are we dead are we still alive
is this where time ends is there time somewhere else
people are only here on earth
with pungent flowers and with songs
and out of the world
surely
they make truths!

only we come to make songs on earth
to know each other in the place of drums
you are a friend!
nothing is so far away
and nothing breaks

nothing is so precious nothing so strong
as the giver of life
eagle that goes flying
tiger heart of the mountain
now the yellow tiger is crying
now the claws of the white eagle hiss

I am nothing more than a singer
flower is my heart
I give you my song
everything I was is here
my fan my feathers my scents
my bent cane flower of paper
in the house of sea moss
in the house of light

Oh gods makers of life
where do you live
deep inside the sky
you carry this city in your arms
in your endless hands

beat the great drum
it is the drum that gives life
the king the god
a little time
here

Oh never never die
drum and songmakers of life!
yes merely men
for a while
and the earth
Oh god where are your flowers
will we take them to your house
are we going to leave them
on the faces of the dead

in the room of yellow feathers
in the room of green birds
you are
happy there there we look for
your word Oh
giver

the flowers have come
the spring flowers crackling like the sun
all these petals your heart your body
Oh you through whom everyone lives
I give the world my flowers
I drink their honey
they are his flowers god
opens them
flowers of snow in his house
touch them

flowers of red and blue
mix with flowers of fiery red
it is your word your heart
Oh my king
for a little while I can see earth
I cry because death kills
everything I did
everything I sang
for a little while I can see the earth

now in spring we are moving
in the middle of the plains
the tree blue green red
blows over us like a storm
a face in the face of water
now the four corners of the world
flash out of them cool winds of rain
flowers that were dry
the first Mexicans passing

just like the flowers I will go
my fame will be nothing
someday
nothing of my name will be left
to the last flower the last song

where are you my god
so many times I have looked for you
for you I am a sad singer
white heavyscented flowers rain down
only drunken white flowers
in the house of spring
in the house of color upon color

you have come
roots of the blossoming trees
in my nostrils I
am happy
sweet tastes on my lips

now my friends
listen
the dream I am singing
is
each spring life
in the corn
put on a collar of rare stones

you who give life
worshiped with flowers
we kneel down we please you
between drums draped with flowers
Oh king of the Palace of Waters
all the great gods live in your faith
the masters
sigh through flowers

my soul fills to the brim with what I say
Oh friends
I am going to let my heart roam the earth
looking for peace
looking for good luck
no one is born twice

in vain friends
cheerfully
take your bells
throw flowers walk
here we lift new songs
here new flowers fill our hands
no bitterness no sadness
no one be sad! no one remember the earth!
flowers words
we touch each other
friends
we have to leave beautiful
SONGS!
we have to leave beautiful
FLOWERS!

is the word of god with us
on earth
it is the book of your heart
it is your song

I have tasted the wine of mushrooms and my
       heart screams
anguish I am lost
I hate death nothing is true
nothing is left

where is there no death
will I go there
mother in the place of mystery
father in the place of mystery
my heart stops NOT DEATH NO!
I am terrified!

my mouth is full of cries
your flowers your songs
cover the place of mystery
heart
is the truth inside you

I see eagles tigers I see glory
but I am sad leaving the friendship
that we have here

cheerfully sing cheerfully
Oh singer
love it here
now give joy to the giver of life

Oh nothing will cut down the flower of war
there it is on the edges of the river
here it is opening its petals
flower of the tiger flower of the shield
dust rises over the bells

a piece of fallen jade
a flower shoots up
it is your song

many pictures my heart
many songs
I come to give pleasure I come
to relive what gives life
here over the strewn mat
red-throated flowers open

I am here! I am here!
I come from the sea from the middle of the waters
there the water darkens itself
its colors
dawn

drink honey
your heart opens with each drop
it is a flower!

between cactus and acacia
both
other acacias other cactuses
now this giant earth is empty
dust
in our houses
the sound of the flowers that listen
the sound of the songs that hear

3 | *Paz to Annensky*

Altar of the Sun | OCTAVIO PAZ

La treizième revient…c'est encore la première;
et c'est toujours la seule — ou c'est le seul moment;
car es-tu reine, o toi, la première ou dernière?
es-tu roi, toi le seul ou le dernier amant?
— GERARD DE NERVAL, *Arthemis*

A willow of crystal, a black aspen of water,
A tall spout bent by the wind,
A dancer with its roots in tight,
A rivery promenade that curves,
Advances, cuts back, spirals,
And always becomes:
                              a quiet lane
Of stars or leisurely April,
Water oozing prophecies
All night long through closed eyelids,
Unanimous ghost in the groundswell,
Wave after wave until everything is under it,
Green kingdom without end
Like the dazzle of wings
When wings open in the center of the sky,
A trail through the underbrush
Of days to come and the doomed
Radiance of a dying man, like a wood thrush
Freezing the grove with its tune,
Good luck up ahead
Among dividing and vanishing branches,
Hours of light already pecked by the birds,
Omens that trickle through our fingers,
A phantom of unexpected song,
Like wind chanting in the fire,
An endless gaze that balances high
The whole world, its oceans and hills,

Body of light filtered through agate,
Thighs of light, belly of light, harbors,
Ignited cliff, body tinted with clouds
The color of quick, pouncing day,
The hour glitters and has flesh,
Now the world is visible through your body,
Transparent through your transparency.

I wander between lanes of noises,
I flow among resonant ghosts,
I tap through transparencies like the blind,
A reflection blazes me away,
I come to life in someone else,
Ah, forest of haunted columns,
Under the arches of light I enter
The porches of autumnal gauze,

I pace your body as if it were the earth,
Your belly is a bronzed courtyard,
Your breasts two churches where clandestine
Metaphors king the blood,
My gazes cover you like ivy,
You are a city bombarded by the sea,
A barricade which the light halves
In sections the color of a peach tree,
A couple made of salt, rocks, and birds.
Ruled by the astonished noon.

Clothed in the flush of my hungers
You walked naked like my meditations,
I swim through your eyes as if they were water,
Tigers guzzle sleep in those eyes,
The hummingbird chars itself in those flames,
I pass through your brow as if it were the moon,

Like a cloud through your mind,
I drift through your belly as if it were your dreams,

Your skirt of corn ripples and sings,
Your skirt of crystal, your skirt of water,
Your lips, your hair, your glances,
All night you rain, all day long
You free my chest with your fingers of water,
Close my eyes with your mouth of water,
Soak my bones, in my chest
You sink a liquid tree with little roots of water,

I cross your shape as if it were a river,
I ramble through your body as if it were a wood,
A mountain path
Ending in a sudden hole,
I climb your honed reveries
And at the exit of your white forehead
My shadow spills over a cliff and wrecks itself,
I gather my fragments one by one
And walk on without a body, dazed, exploring

Incessant corridors of memory,
Doors left open on a vacant ballroom
Where all summers rot,
Rubies of thirst blaze at the bottom,
My face dissolves when I remember it,
My hand falls apart if I touch it,
Hair of turbulent spiders
Over very old smiles,

At the exit of my forehead I search,
I search without finding, I rummage an instant,
A face of lightning and agony

Running among the evening trees.
Face of rain in a dark garden,
Obstinate water that flows to my side,
I hunt for nothing, I write in private,
No one is here, the day falls, the year falls,
I go down with the moment, hitting the bottom,
Invisible, I cruise over mirrors
Etching my ruined image,
I trample days, minutes in transit,
I tread the daydreams of my shadow,
I pace my shadow in search of an instant,
I seek a live date like a dove,
I look for the five o'clock sun
Warmed by the fences of shale:
The hour ripens its clusters
And when they explode, little girls emerge,
Rise from the cold rose-colored guts of time, and scatter
Through the stone patios of the academy,
Wild hour, like autumn riding high
Sheathed with light under the arcades
While space fits it with a gown
Of transparent, thickly gilded leather,

Tiger the color of light, brown stag
In the vicinity of the night,
Vague, lounging girl
On the green balconies of rain,
Adolescent with over a million faces,
I have forgotten your name, Melusina,
Laura, Isabel, Proserpine, Maria,
You have every face and not one of them,
You are all hours and none of them,
You look like the pine and the cloud,
You are every bird and a planet,

You seem to be the blade of a sword
And near the hangman's cup of blood,
Ivy advancing, you dress and dismantle
The soul, dividing it,
Text of the fire over jade,
Groove in the cliff, queen of snakes,
Pillar of mist, fountain in the rock,
Carnival on the moon, boulder of eagles,
Grain of anise, diminishing thorn
And mortal who inflicts continuous pain,
Caretaker of the valleys undersea
And shepherd of the dead's glen,
Rope of grass hung from the sheer peak of dizziness,
Vine, poisonous hedge,
Blossom of resurrection, grape of life,

Lady of the flute and the lightning,
Terrace of jasmine, salt in the wound,
Bunch of roses for the firing squad,
Snow in August, executioner's moon,
Document of sea over the dark marble,
Inscription of wind in the desert,
Testament of the sun, pomegranate, tassel,
Face of flames, eaten head,
Hunted, teenage face
Counterfeit years, Ferris wheel days
Facing the same courtyard, the same wall,
The moment glows,
The successive masks of the flames are only one face,
All names are a single name,
All faces one face,
All ages are a single instant
And for every century of centuries
One pair of eyes closes the road to the future,

There is nothing in front of me but a split second,
Ransomed tonight, held against a dream,
A dream made of welded reveries,
Etched deep against the dream,
Torn from the nothing of this night,
Wrestled and erected letter by letter,
While in the open, time runs wild
And the world, with its carnivorous fist of hours,
Batters the gates of my soul
Just for a second, while cities,
Names, flavors, everything vivid,
Crumble in my blind forehead,
While the massive grief of the night
Crushes my thought and my skeleton,
And my blood runs down, slows,
And my teeth wobble and my eyes
Fog and the days and the years
Pile up their empty terrors,

While time shuts its fan
And nothing happens behind its images
The moment hugs itself and floats,
Inspecting death, menacing
Throughout the night's dismal yawn,
Adrift in the slang
Of active death, the moment
In masquerade hugs itself, loves itself
Like a fist closing, a plum
Ripening privately,
Drinks itself and, brimming over,
The translucent instant looks
And grows inwardly, puts down tiny roots,
Swells inside me, makes itself at home,
I cough up its delirious leaves,
My thoughts are only its birds,

Its mercury circulates through my veins,
Mental tree, fruits tasting of time,

Oh life made for living, already lived,
Time turned head over heels in a surf
Dives down without showing its face,
What passed never was, but is passing
And noiselessly flows into
Another disappearing instant:
Across from the afternoon of rock salt and stone,
A red illegible writing,
Armed with invisible razors,
Scribbles on my skin and those wounds
Revive me like a jacket of flames,
Fierce but not fatal, I look for water,
There is no water in your eyes, they are stone,
And your breasts, your belly, your hips,
Are stone, your mouth tastes like dust,
Sometimes it reeks of cyanide,
Your body tastes like a deep pit with no way out,
Alley of mirrors echoing
The eyes of anxiety, hall
That always veers at the point of parting,
I'm blind, and you take me by the hand
Through those violent galleries

To the center of the circle where you straighten up
Like a flare congealing into a touch,
A light that flays, fascinating
Like the stage of the damned,
Flexible as a whip, slender, handsome,
Like the twin arm of the moon,
And your iron phrases break
Open my chest, empty my streets and spill out,
You rip memories out of me one by one,

I have lost my name, my friends
Grumble among pigs or rot
In the teeth of a violent sun,

I'm filled with a long wound,
A gulley no one crosses,
Phantom of braille, thinking
That swerves, echoes, reflects itself
And gets lost in its own transparency,
Conscience pierced by an eye
Watching itself until it drowns
In brightness:
            I see your horrible armor,
Melusina, brilliantly greenish at dawn,
You sleep twisted among the sheets,
Waking up, you scream like a bird
And fall eternally, broken and white,
Nothing remains but your cry,
And at the end of the centuries I find myself
With a cough, nearsighted, shuffling
Faded snapshots:
              there is no one, you are no one,
A mound of ashes, a broom.
A rusty knife and a feather,
A skin full of bones hung up to dry,
A wrinkled cluster now, a black hole —
At the bottom, the eyes of a baby girl
Drowned for a thousand years,

Glances buried in a well,
Gazes that watch us from the world's beginning,
Girlish stare of the old mother
Who sees a young father in the grown boy,
Mother's gaze of the only girl
Who sees a little son in the tall father,

144

Such gazes that look at us from the bottom
Of life are snares of the dead
— or is it the reverse: we find the true life again
When we drop into those eyes?

To fall, come back, dream, while other
Eyes in the future dream of me, another life,
Other clouds, to die another death,
Oh tonight, tonight is enough, and this instant
Has just blossomed, it shows me
Where I was, who I was, what your name is,
What I call myself:
               did I make plans
For the summer — for every summer —
On Christopher Street, ten years ago,
With Phyllis who had two dimples
Where the sparrows drank light?
On the Reforma, Carmen said to me
"Don't weigh the air, it's always October here,"
Or did she tell someone else I lost it all
Or imagined it, without telling me?
Did I travel by night to Oaxaca,
Immense and lush like a tree,
Talking to myself, a gust of nonsensical wind,
And when I got back to my room — always a room —
Did the mirrors know me?
From the Hotel Vernet did we watch the dawn
Dance with a chestnut tree — "Now it's very late,"
You said, fixing your hair, and did I find
Stains on the wall, and keep my mouth shut?
Did we climb the tower hand in hand, did we see
The afternoon drop to the stone road,
Did we eat grapes in Bidart? Did we buy
Gardenias in Perote?
               names, places,

Streets and boulevards, faces, courtyards, roads,
Seasons, a park, lonely rooms,
Streaks on the wall, someone combing,
Someone humming at my side, someone who sees,
Rooms, towns, streets, names, rooms,

Madrid, 1937,
In the Square of the Angel women
Wove and sang with their sons,
Later the alarm rang, red cries,
Homes kneeling in the dust,
Cracked turrets, pimply foreheads,
The hurricane of motors, held back, motionless:
They undressed and made love
To defend our eternal portion,
Our ration of time and paradise,
To touch our very roots and revive us,
Refresh our heritage carried off
By robbers of life for a thousand centuries,
They undressed and kissed
Because, naked, close together,
They leave time behind, they become invulnerable,
Nothing touches them, they go back to the root,
There is neither you nor I, tomorrow, yesterday, names,
The truth of the couple with only a body and a soul,
Oh to be whole...
                    rooms adrift
Among cities living in danger,
Rooms and avenues, names like scars,
The room with windows on other rooms
With the same crummy wallpaper

Where a man in shirtsleeves reads the news
Or a woman irons, the neat room
Which the boughs of the peach tree visit,

The other room, outside it always rains,
There's a yard and three rusty children,
these rooms are cruisers that sway
In a gulf of light, or submarines:
The quiet scatters in green waves,
Everything we touch gleams,
Vaults of luxury, the portraits
Poor now, threadbare the rugs,
Trapdoors, cells, enchanted caves,
Bird watchers and numbered rooms,
Everything is transfigured, everything flutters,
Each molding is a cloud, each door
Leads to the sea, to the fields, the air, each table
Is a feast, time harmlessly
Charges them, these locked conchs,
Now there is no time, no wall: space, space,
Open your hand, seize this treasure,
Pick the fruits, eat life,
Stretch out at the foot of the tree, drink the water!

Everything is changed, everything sacred,
Each room is the hub of the world,
The first night, the first day,
The world is born when a couple kisses,
Glassy entrails of a drop of light
The room half-opens like a shy gourd
Or explodes like a speechless planet,
And the eating habits of mice,
The gratings of the banks and jails,
The bars of paper, the wire fences,
The stamps and the fang of time, the false victory,
The monotonous lecture of guns,
The gentle scorpion wearing a bonnet,
The tiger sporting a silk hat, president
Of the Vegetarians' Club and the Red Cross,

The pedagogical donkey, the crocodile
Dressed like Messiah, father of populations,
The Chief, the shark, the architect
Of the future, the uniformed pig,
The favorite son of the Church
Who cleans his black dentures
With holy water and takes classes
In English and Democracy, the invisible
Walls, the rotten masks
Dividing the man from men,
The man from himself,

                    they wallow
In a great moment, and we get a glimpse
Of our lost brotherhood, the weakness
That means we are men, the glory of being men,
The chance to share bread, sun, death,
The forgotten dread of being alive:
To love is to fight, if two people kiss
The world changes, desire comes to life,
Thought walks, wings bud
In the shoulders of the slave, the world
Is real, tangible, wine is wine,
You can taste bread again, water is water,
To live is to fight, to open doors,
To stop being a ghost with a number
Perpetuating a damned chain
Through loves without a face;

                    the world changes
If two people look up and recognize each other,
To love is to take off your names:
"Let me be your whore," are the words
Of Eloise, but you go along with the law,
You marry her and in return
They castrate you later;

                    better the felony,

The suicidal lovers, the incest
Of brothers, two mirrors
In love with their likeness,
Better to munch poisoned bread,

The adulterer in beds of ash,
Ferocious loves, delirium,
Your poison ivy the sodomite
Who wears a carnation of phlegm
Pinned on his lapel,
Better to be stoned to death
In the squares winding to the draw-well
That slowly oozes the fluid of life,
Eternity changes in empty hours,
Minutes jailed, time
Stamped in pennies and odorless turds;
Better chastity, hidden lily
That sways on the trunks of silence,
The tough diamond of the saints
That filters desire, quenching it at the same time,
Weddings of tranquility and movement,
The solitude sings in its halo,
Each hour is a petal of crystal,
The world unmasks
And at its core, joyous lucidity,
The One we call God, being without a name,
He contemplates, at home in the void,
Being without a face,
He comes from himself, sun or suns,
Abundance of presences and names;

I follow my madness, rooms, streets,
I walk the staircase of time with my arms outstretched,
I climb over and under its rungs,
I touch its walls and stand still,

I end where I begin, I hunt your face,
I wander through the streets of my being
Under an ageless sun, at my side, you
Prance like a tree, like a river,
You grow like cornsilk between my fingers,
You throb like a squirrel in my palms,
You soar like a sky of birds, your laugh
Has covered me with foam, your head
Is a small comet between my hands,
The world gets green again if you smile,
Eating an orange,
                                    the earth is new
If two people, dizzy, holding each other,
Loll in the grass: the sky falls,
The trees take off, space
Is only light and silence, space alone
Opens for the eye's eagle,
Overhead, a white tribe of clouds goes by,
The body's cables break, the soul weighs anchor,
We lose our names and drift
Floating between the blue and the green,
Time is complete, where nothing passes
But your own appropriate, happy lapse of time,

Nothing happens, silence, blinkings,
(Silence: an angel crosses this huge moment
Like the life of a hundred suns),
Is this blinking all that happens?
—And the banquet, the exile, the first crime,
The mule's jawbone, the dense noise,
The skeptical gaze of the dead
When they drop to the red, ash-colored plain,
Agamemnon's immense bellow,
Cassandra's repeated cry
More poignant than the waves breaking,

Socrates in chains (the sun rises,
Dying is waking: "Crito, a rooster
To Aesculapius, full of life now")
The jackal chattering among the ruins
Of Nineveh, the shadow that rapes Brutus
Before the battle, Moctezuma
Wracked by insomnia's bed of thorns,
The journey to death made by the gallows cart,
The endless excursion, minute by minute,
But rarely for Robespierre,
The broken jaw held in the hands,
Churruca in his winecask like a scarlet throne,
For Lincoln, on his way to the theatre,
Only a few steps left,
The rattle in Trotsky's throat, his moans
Of a wild boar, Madero and his gaze
Which no one questioned: "Why do they kill me?"
The yells, the yeses, the silences
Of the criminal, the saint, the poor devil,
Graveyards of phrases and anecdotes
Scrawled by rhetorical dogs,
Delirium, whining, the dark noise
We make when we die and that murmur
Of life called birth, the snap
Of crushed bones in a scuffle
The prophet's foaming mouth
His outcry, the grunt of the hangman
And the wail of the victim...
                              they are flames,
The eyes are flame, flames whatever they see,
Flame the ear and the sound flame,
White coal the lips, the tongue a branding iron,
The touch and what is touched, thinking
And what's thought, flame is the object pondered,
Everything burns, the universe is flame,

The very same nothing burns, it is not nothing
But a thought in flames, smoke finally:
There is no executioner, no victim...

                                                         what about the cry
On Friday afternoon? and the silence
Speaking without words, doesn't it say anything?
Are the cries of men nothing,
Does nothing happen when time passes?

—Nothing happens, only a wink
Of sun, a trivial gesture, nothing,
There's no redemption, time doesn't run backwards,
The dead are frozen in their death,
They can't die another death,
Untouchables, trapped in their frown,
From their solitude, from their grave,
Incurables, they watch us without seeing us,
Now their death is the statue of their life,
Infinite noun of nothing, always nothing,
A phantom King ruling your banter
And your last reflex, a fine mask
Decorating your mobile face:
We are becoming the monument of a life
Owned by others, dim, scarcely ours,

— Life, when was it really ours?
When are we really what we are?
We don't take a good look, in private
We're nothing but dizzy, empty,
Grins, leers in the mirror — horror and vomit,
Life is never ours, others own it,
Life is nobody's, all of us
Are life — bread of the sun for others,
All those others we are —,
I'm someone else when I am, my acts

Are more mine if they are everyone's as well,
In order to exist I have to be someone else,
Leave myself, look for myself among others,
The others who are not if I do not exist,
Others who give me total existence,
I am not, there is no I, we are always ourselves,
Life is other, always over there, more distant,
Outside of you, of me, constantly on the horizon,
Life wants us, throws us out,
Builds a face for us, then eats it,
Hunger of being, oh death, everyone's bread,
Eloise, Proserpine, Maria,
When will you show your face and see
My real face, my face belonging to someone else,
My face of Us, always everyone else's,
Face of tree and of baker,
Of chauffeur, of cloud and of ocean,
Face of sun and stream and Pedro and Pablo,
Face of every solitary person,
Wake me, now I am born:

Face of sea, of bread, of rock and fountain,
Flowing that dissolves our faces
In the face without a name, the faceless being,
Inexpressible presence of presences...

I want to continue, go deeper, but I can't:
This instant plunges from one to another,
I had dreams of dreamless stone
And at the end of the years like stones
I heard my circling blood sing,
With a rumble of light the sea sang,
One by one the walls fell down,
Each door decayed,
The sun entered and plundered my skull,

My closed eyelids opened,
My being broke free of your skin,
I dug myself up, I quarried
Ages of stone from my brute sleep
And your magic of mirrors rebuilt
A willow of crystal, a black aspen of water,
A tall spout bent by the wind,
A dancer with its roots in tight,
A rivery promenade that curves,
Advances, cuts back, spirals,
And always becomes:

Clouded Sky | MIKLÓS RADNÓTI

The moon hangs on a clouded sky.
I am surprised that I live.
Anxiously and with great care, death looks for us
and those it finds are all terribly white.

Sometimes a year looks back and howls
then drops to its knees.
Autumn is too much for me. It waits again
and winter waits with its dull pain.

The forest bleeds. The hours bleed.
Time spins overhead
and the wind scrawls
big dark numbers on the snow.

But I am still here
and I know why and why the air feels heavy —
a warm silence full of tiny noises circles me
just as it was before my birth.

I stop at the foot of a tree.
Its leaves cry with anger.
A branch reaches down. Is it strangling me?
I am not a coward, I am not weak, I am

tired. And silent. And the branch
is also mute and afraid as it enters my hair.
I should forget it, but I
forget nothing.

Clouds pour across the moon. Anger
leaves a poisonous dark green bruise on the sky.
I roll myself a cigarette,
slowly, carefully. I live.

June 8, 1940

Song | MIKLÓS RADNÓTI

Whipped by sorrow now
each day I walk
exiled in my own country

and it barely matters how long or where.
I come, go, sit,
and even the distant stars
descend and attack me.

Even the distant stars
hide behind clouds.
I stumble through the night
to the shores where reeds grow.

Where reeds grow
nobody walks with me now
and I haven't really wanted
to dance for a long time.

For a long time now the deer
with the chilly nose hasn't followed me.
I wade through a swamp,
mist curls up from its surface,

mist curls up from its surface
and I sink, and sink.
Above me, a pair of
hawks hangs like wet rags.

June 7, 1939

Two Fragments | MIKLÓS RADNÓTI

I

The evening splashed down and the high trees
swam away in it. Behind the fog
the waking Great Bear growled.

It grew dark. I don't see you here
although you stand beside me under this branch
then fly up, opening your wings.

You don't have a body now. Are you an angel?
You leave me here, but it doesn't matter. I know you'll be back.
Don't you even have a body now? The fog drizzles on you too,
turning the hair on your forehead gray.

2

And like brown coal rooted in the deepest mines
the branch hides in the fog,
bending occasionally, leaving one or two cool
dark drops on my face.

Think — the other side of the fog! I shiver,
I should be happy, now that the world is bandaged with fog
and I see nothing. Nothing?

For no reason the bright smell of mushrooms, everything
there is, comforts me. O God,
the fog curls around me! For no reason

I stand in the cool rotting leaves
among my unwinding visions.

November 23, 1939

Fires | MIKLÓS RADNÓTI

Fires break out and slowly die forever.
Soldiers' ghosts fly to the bright meridians. One soul!
Oh, it doesn't matter who this one or that one was
while the heat bends repeatedly here, and the frost screams there.
Sailors at the guns of torn ships, drunk on homesickness,
vomiting in their yellow fear.
Mines burst everywhere, death watches carefully,
and sometimes at high tide, with a slippery body, it crawls ashore.
Dead men follow it. Dolphins are ripped apart.
Dawn wakes too but no one needs it.
A plane roars across. Its shadow
follows it silently on the fox-eyed sea.
A whirlpool breathes, signals cross on the water,
blood flowers on the reef instead of coral,
the plague howls all day, oil leaks over the fire engines,
insanity and fear hide behind them.
Then the sun drowns in smoke and, like a long-stemmed pain,
the moon quivers repeatedly on the other side
and fires break out, and slowly die forever.
Soldiers' ghosts fly to the bright meridians.

December 20, 1939

With Your Right Hand on the Back of My Head

| MIKLÓS RADNÓTI

I lay at night with your right hand on the back of my head,
daytime still hurt because I asked you not to take it away.
I listened to the blood circling in your neck.

It was around twelve and sleep weighed me down,
it fell as suddenly as it did years ago, in
my drowsy, woolly childhood, and it rocked me as gently.

You tell me that it wasn't even three o'clock
when I woke terrified and sat up
and mumbled and recited poems and howled incoherently.

I spread my arms out the way a bird ruffled by fear
beats its wings when a shadow curves in the garden.
I was planning to go, but where? What kind of death shook me?
Dear, you tried to quiet me and I, sleeping as I sat, let you.
I lay back silently. The road of terrors waited.
And I kept on dreaming. Maybe about a different death.

April 6, 1941

Metaphors | MIKLÓS RADNÓTI

You are like a whispering branch
when you bend over me,
or like the secret taste
of a poppy —

and like ripples continually forming in time
you excite me,
and quiet me
like stone on top of a grave.

You are like a friend I grew up with,
and even today I don't really know
the smell
of your thick hair.

Sometimes when you look sad, I'm afraid
you'll leave me, like
coiled drifting smoke, and sometimes when
you're the color of lightning, I'm afraid of you —

like the sky exploding when the sun
burns it dark gold.
And when you're angry, you
are like the letter "u,"

deep-voiced, vibrating again and again,
and dark. At times like these
I take smiles
and draw bright nooses around you.

November 16, 1941

Charm | MIKLÓS RADNÓTI

With trembling eyes
I sit in the light
a rose tree jumps
over the hedge
the light jumps too
clouds gather
lightning flashes
and already high up
wild thunder
answers
wild thunder
down below the blue
of lakes withers
the surfaces flood
come into the house
take off your dress
it's raining outside now
take off your shirt
let the rain wash
our hearts into one heart.

February 1, 1942

I Hid You | MIKLÓS RADNÓTI

I hid you for a long time
the way a branch hides its
slowly ripening fruit among leaves,
and like a flower of sane ice
on a winter window
you open in my mind.
Now I know what it means
when your hand swoops up to your hair.
In my heart I keep
the small tilt of your ankle too
and I'm amazed by the delicate curve
of your ribs, coldly,
like someone who has lived
such breathing miracles.
Still, in my dreams
often I have a hundred arms
and like God
I hold you in those arms.

February 20, 1942

Suddenly | MIKLÓS RADNÓTI

Suddenly at night the wall moves,
silence breaks into the heart, and the word breaks out.
The rib twinges. Familiar with grief, the pulse under the
      bone fades.
Silently the body rises. Only the wall is heard.
And the heart, the hand and the mouth know that this is death,
      this is death.
This is prison when the lights fade.
Inside the convicts know, outside the guards know too
that the current all comes together in one body.
The lightbulb is quiet, a shadow rushes through the cell,
and then the guards, the convicts and the bugs, smell the odor of
      scorched human flesh.

April 20, 1942

Night | MIKLÓS RADNÓTI

The heart sleeps, and fear sleeps in the heart.
The fly sleeps near the cobweb on the wall.
It is quiet in the house,
the wakeful mouse is quiet,
the garden sleeps, the branch,
the woodpecker in the tree,
the bee in the hive, the chafer in the rose.
The summer sleeps in the spinning grains of wheat,
fire sleeps in the moon,
there is a cold medal on the sky.
Autumn wakes. It goes stealing in the night.

June 1, 1942

Hesitating Ode | MIKLÓS RADNÓTI

I've been planning to tell you
about the secret galaxy of my love for so long —
in just one image, just the essence.
But you are swarming and flooding inside me like
existence, as eternal and certain sometimes
as a snail shell changed to stone inside a stone.
Spattered by the moon, night curves over my head
and hunts for the little dreams that rustle
suddenly, then take flight. But I still can't
tell you what it really means to me when I write
and feel your warm glance above my hands.
Metaphors are useless. They come up. I drop them.
And tomorrow I'll begin the whole thing over again
because I'm worth about as much as the words
in this poem and because all this excites me until
I'm only bone and a few tufts of hair.
You are tired. I feel it too. It was a long day.
What else can I say? Objects look at each other
and praise you, half a cube of sugar sings
on the table, drops of honey fall and
glow on the tablecloth like beads of pure gold.
An empty glass clinks by itself,
happy because it lives with you. And maybe I'll
have time to tell you what it's like when it waits
for you to come back. Dreaming's slowly falling
darkness touches, touches me, flies off, then touches
your brow again. Your heavy lids say good-bye.
Your hair spreads out and flickers
and you sleep. The long shadow of your eyelashes
quivers. Your hand sinks on
my pillow, a birch branch going to sleep.

But I sleep in you also. You aren't "another" world.
And I can hear how the many mysterious,
thin, wise lines change

in your cool palm.

May 26, 1943

Unnoticed | MIKLÓS RADNÓTI

You drift from youth into manhood
as unnoticed as if you were drifting off to sleep.
You have a past, you sit around facing bottles of hard liquor,
and more and more of your friends become fathers.

Now, the father comes to see you with his little son,
and pretty soon the boy understands you better,
he understands the burning adventures of your heart,
and playing on the floor, together you outwit the seesaw of time.

But the day comes when you make money like a grownup,
you translate on commission, sell poems,
argue about contracts, calculate, protest,
and you too can only make a living with the help of "extras."

You don't look for success, you know it doesn't help.
That lady favors only those who exist at the right time —
You like the poppy and the red-skinned sour cherry
instead of the honey and walnut which fascinate sad teenagers.

And you know that in summer too a leaf can fall,
no matter how much the brain burns and dances,
and that everything will be measured when you're dead.
You can't be a great athlete or a roaming sailor,

but you have learned that the pen is a weapon and a tool
and you can break your neck trying to write an honest poem
and you know this way too you can reach all those places
where intentions are bare and the fires of adventure burn.

And as you write, pressing your weight on the pen, you think
about children, and there is no pride in your sad heart.
You work for them, for those in factories, creaking with
silent dust, for those in workshops who are bending their backs.

November 15, 1943

I Don't Know | MIKLÓS RADNÓTI

I don't know what this land means to others, this little country
circled by fire, place of my birth,
world of my childhood, rocking in the distance.
I grew out of her like the fragile branch of a tree,
and I hope my body will sink down in her.
Here, I'm at home. When, one by one, bushes kneel at my feet,
I know their names and the names of their flowers.
I know people who walk down the roads, know where
    they're going,
and on a summer evening, I know the meaning of pain
that turns red and trickles down the walls of houses.
This land is only a map for the pilot who flies over.
He doesn't know where the poet Vörösmarty lived.
For him factories and angry barracks hide on this map.
For me there are grasshoppers, oxen, church steeples, gentle farms.
Through binoculars, he sees factories and plowed fields,
I see the worker, shaking, afraid for his work.
I see forests, orchards filled with song, vineyards, graveyards,
and a little old woman who weeps and weeps quietly among
    the graves.
The industrial plant and the railway must be destroyed.
But it's only a watchman's box where a man stands outside
sending messages with a red flag. There are children around him,
in the factory yard a sheepdog plays, rolling on the ground.
And there's the park and the footprints of lovers from the past.
Sometimes kisses tasted like honey, sometimes like blackberries.
I didn't want to take a test one day, so on my way to school
I tripped on a stone at the edge of the sidewalk.
Here is the stone, but from up there it can't be seen.
There's no instrument to show it all.
We're sinners, just like people everywhere,
we know what we did wrong, when and how and where.
But innocent workers and poets live here too.

Knowledge grows inside nursing babies,
it shines in there. Hiding in dark cellars, they guard it,
waiting for the day when the finger of peace will mark our land.
And their new words will answer our muffled ones.

Night cloud, you who stay awake, spread your great wings over us.

January 17, 1944

In Hiding | MIKLÓS RADNÓTI

I look at the mountain from the window,
it does not see me.
I hide, I write a poem,
not that it matters,
and I see the old grace. It is useless.
As before, the moon cuts into the sky
and the cherry opens.

May 9, 1944

Picnic in May | MIKLÓS RADNÓTI

The noise of the record player in the grass,
hoarse, breathless, hunted —
but there are no hunters here
only girls circling it
like fiery flowers.

A little girl falls on her knees.
She changes the record.
Her back is brown, her legs white.
The music is bad
but her child's soul rises anyway.
It is gray, like clouds.

There are boys crouching. Awkward pretty words
stick to their lips like embers.
Their bodies swell with many little victories.
Calmly, when they have to,
they kill.

But they can still be men.
What is human about them sleeps
somewhere inside.
Say it, say that there is hope.

May 10, 1944

Fragment | MIKLÓS RADNÓTI

I lived on this earth in an age
when man fell so low
he killed willingly, for pleasure, without orders.
Mad obsessions threaded his life,
he believed in false gods. Deluded, he foamed at the mouth.

I lived on this earth in an age
when honor was betrayal and murder,
the traitor and the thief were heroes —
those who were silent, unwilling to rejoice,
were hated as if they had the plague.

I lived on this earth in an age
when if a man spoke out, he had to go into hiding
and could only chew his fists in shame —
drunk on blood and scum, the nation went mad
and grinned at its horrible fate.

I lived on this earth in an age
when a curse was the mother of a child,
when women were happy if they miscarried,
a glass of thick poison foamed on the table,
and the living envied the rotting silence of the dead.

I lived on this earth in an age
when the poets too were silent
and waited for Isaiah, the scholar
of terrifying words, to speak again —
since only he could utter the right curse.

May 19, 1944

Root | MIKLÓS RADNÓTI

Power glides in the root,
drinking rain, living in the earth,
and its dream is white snow.

From underneath it rises and breaks through
the soil and crawls along secretly.
Its arm is like rope.

On the root's arm a worm sleeps
and a worm sticks to its leg.
The world is rotten with worms.

But the root goes on living below.
It is the branch, heavy with leaves,
that it lives for, not the world.

This is what it feeds and loves,
sending delicate tastes up to it,
sweet tastes out of the sky.

I am a root myself now,
living among worms.
This poem is written down there.

I was a flower. I became a root.
There is heavy black earth above me.
The workers on my life are done.
A saw wails over my head.

Lager Heidenau, in the
mountains above Zagubica,
August 8, 1944

Forced March | MIKLÓS RADNÓTI

You're crazy. You fall down,   stand up and walk again,
your ankles and your knees move   pain that wanders around,
but you start again   as if you had wings.
The ditch calls you, but it's no use   you're afraid to stay,
and if someone asks why,   maybe you turn around and say
that a woman and a sane death   a better death wait for you.
But you're crazy.   For a long time now
only the scorched wind spins   above the houses at home.
Walls lie on their backs,   plum trees are broken
and the angry night   wails with fear.
Oh, if I could believe   that everything valuable
is not only inside me now   that there's still home to go back to.
If only there were! And just as before   bees drone peacefully
on the cool veranda,   plum preserves turn cold
and over sleepy gardens   quietly the end of summer bathes in
        the sun.
Among the leaves the fruit   swings naked
and in front of the rust-brown hedge   blond Fanny waits for me,
the morning writes   slow shadows —
All this could happen!   The moon is so round today!
Don't walk past me, friend.   Yell, and I'll stand up again!

September 15, 1944

Postcard | MIKLÓS RADNÓTI

I

From Bulgaria the huge wild pulse of artillery.
It beats on the mountain ridge, then hesitates and falls.
Men, animals, wagons, and thoughts. They are swelling.
The road whinnies and rears up. The sky gallops.
You are permanent within me in this chaos.
Somewhere deep in my mind you shine forever, without
moving, silent, like the angel awed by death,
or like the insect burying itself
in the rotted heart of a tree.

In the mountains

Postcard | MIKLÓS RADNÓTI

2

Nine miles from here
the haystacks and houses burn,
and on the edges of the meadow
there are quiet frightened peasants, smoking.
The little shepherd girl seems
to step into the lake, the water ripples.
The ruffled sheepfold
bends to the clouds and drinks.

Cservenka, October 6, 1944

Postcard | MIKLÓS RADNÓTI

3

Bloody drool hangs on the mouths of the oxen.
The men all piss red.
The company stands around in stinking wild knots.
Death blows overhead, disgusting.

Mohacs, October 24, 1944

Postcard | MIKLÓS RADNÓTI

4

I fell next to him. His body rolled over.
It was tight as a string before it snaps.
Shot in the back of the head — "This is how
you'll end." "Just lie quietly," I said to myself.
Patience flowers into death now.
"Der springt noch auf," I heard above me.
Dark filthy blood was drying on my ear.

Szentkirályszabadja,
October 31, 1944

Thirst | URI ZVI GREENBERG

I need water not wine
or drugs,
I want my brain clear until I am that I am.
The line that divides earth nearest the sun is my awareness of being.

I whinnied like a colt in the sun, joy
even at the tip of my shoe broke into me,
spilled over where I put my feet.
Now I know that when joy filled me
it took nothing away from sorrow, it killed,

so now I stare into the mirror like a child many many hours
      and see
someone who watches me in there and
resembles me very closely.

Amputation of the Wing | URI ZVI GREENBERG

Suddenly on a cloudless morning
the odor of plant and beast covered the earth
and each bird had what looked like only one wing, flying...
Pity the man who saw this and didn't take
the grapes of his eyes into his hands and squeeze them!

Even the birds don't know who cut off their wing.
Suddenly they fly like this in the air,
dipping to the left...
Not a drop of blood falls, there isn't a sign that each bird
had two wings once that carried

loving hearts from this place here to that place over there...
Now that place doesn't exist any more.
Like something lost in a dream. God's word has cut off a wing
and He has sealed the place of cutting.

The Tearing of the Mind

URI ZVI GREENBERG

Everybody cries *Money!* even the bums
whose lives go on forever.
The uniformed shitheads who used to police
the Temple are dead,
it's a dump of rotting stones,
people with small eyes use it for a church.
My family's here, donkeys are here,
sheep dung and man dung are here.
Not one prophet sings
in the caves about his vision, only
the radio and the worker speak.
This is a Jewish city.
This is the courtyard of the prison
where the lion that could tell the future
was locked in and eaten by his own fire.
When did it happen? Ask.
Ask the man who pisses against this wall.
This is the blocked Gate of Mercy
timed to split open
stone by stone
when God comes down and faces it
and beats His fists
on the doors until they bleed.
But I won't see Him coming. Here
on the mountain where olives shade the dust,
their sap flowing into the valley up the
other mountainside across from me,
I'll be crumbling bones.
Nothing cools the searing of the mind,
the conscience blazing until
I can't move.

My legs won't hold up my body
and take me away from here,
camels groan, everybody slips money
back and forth, their hands are full of it
one minute, empty the next.
My whole family does it.

The Saying | ERNST STADLER

In an old book
I stumbled across a saying.
It was like a stranger
punching me in the face,

it won't stop
gnawing at me.
When I walk around at night,
looking for a beautiful girl,

when a lie or a description
of life or somebody's fake
way of being with people
occurs instead of reality,

when I betray myself with
an easy explanation
as if what's dark is clear,
as if life doesn't have thousands

of locked, burning gates,
when I use words without really
having known their strict openness
and put my hands around things

that don't excite me,
when a dream hides my face with soft hands
and the day avoids me,
cut off from the world,

cut off from who I am deeply,
I freeze where I am
and see hanging in the air in front of me
STOP BEING A GHOST!

Hear the Mother |

you dream about your own death so you can come home

I always see you I always think about you when I'm asleep like a
   sickness a crow inside me

I'll die without seeing your children thinking about them doesn't
   help can't stop crying

I always compare you to a drifting log with iron nails in it mother
   I always compare you to the sun passing behind clouds
   that's what makes the world dark

you ask me to sing about your mother's death: an eagle took a
   crow over to a good sandy beach to weep but the crow
   always walks up to her and makes her laugh

I hope the shit-eating people whose words have fallen on my
   head eat their own pricks

when I'm drunk I throw everybody's face across the river

I have a great time get drunk fuck swim because I see how people
   treat the dead

the canoe is stuck on the beach my uncle is dead I have to
   forget him

I came here to punch a hole in the big drum to call it a lobster
   and that's what I did

who cares what I lose I only sing to cry about myself

fuck you because you fell down on the beach when you heard
me I don't feel numb anybody who acts like that's blind

you have a nose like a cucumber all bumpy I hate talking to you
you're a slave I hate what you keep saying you can't see
anything don't you know you keep picking up sand instead
of dipping into the cup

I'm like a drum beaten to make peace on the way back

I feel drunk when I think I'm like one of those grass people's
children pity me before I'm sent away

my friend's mind is like mine so I love him I wonder when I
wake up in the morning what I always look for

my own mind is very hard to me it's like I'm carrying around my
mind what's wrong?

Nusni composed this song and immediately after stabbed several
of his friends: he was dreaming of always smiling
everywhere he went

the bear killed all my friends a man like me wanders around this
world somebody else crying he should have all his things
taken away

help me believe when I feel my grandfather's house turning over
inside me can anybody save me?

I love you and I only want to die with you

uncle the noise of your death will come down the Chilkat river
mother the nation's drum has fallen take the drum out take
it away from the nations so they can hear my mother

I always think somewhere deep inside me there's no place people
        don't die

I'm going to bring back everybody and put them in the sun-
        world's houses

master this is how I feel you're joined in me I'm very lonely on
        this trip I'm singing inside I'm crying about myself

this is how I treat myself when my conscience speaks I don't let it
        get past me I see his ghost before he dies

who have I come this far to find? you've moved to another
        town crying

every day I see it I see you when I'm asleep the big black bird crawls
        around inside my chest with an arrow through its neck

this is the big song rich man when you close your eyes you still
        see the sun feel higher than anybody

I think of the future stern of a canoe vanishing around the
        next bend

little children I won't throw your faces away we're friends

now I can see the spirits coming to me half their bodies poke
        through the clouds their feet touch the ground I follow them

my words are like my arms they can make you kneel

the dead get burned smoke rises words can come out any way
        they want to lies go back into the mouth of the man who
        says them like a snake that's why truth is like a child

there is one song sung by the spirits when fire sends them
       food listen

I think of spring what will the days be like little girl I miss you I
       could die with you but nobody can shape death nobody's
       to blame

you turned over you turned the world over how can you
       save yourself?

fish on the beach and snipes what a stink!

I was sitting at my fireplace half-asleep looking into the flames my
       spirit jumped out of the fire and looked back

no one's hand reaches out for me as I drift by the town singing
       you make me feel like I'm shaking thinking about you

I want to tie these around my neck like beads like unborn
       children so they'll be with me when I'm asleep will they
       forgive me?

somebody's using me like a paddle

let's go high up to that cliff you always sleep before you hunt so
       you don't catch a damn thing

I like to creep around under the skirts on my brother's wife and
       look up and

here comes a rich man *shhhhhh* it's all gone

Half of Life | FRIEDRICH HOLDERLÏN

Heavy with yellow pears
and filled with wild roses
the land lies in the sea.
Beautiful swans, drunk on your kisses,
you dip your heads
into the quiet water of saints.

But how shall I find,
when winter comes,
shadows, sunshine,
flowers of the earth?
Cold speechless walls stand there,
weathercocks clatter.

About Me | VLADIMIR MAYAKOVSKY

Children dying make me happy.
Notice: behind my nose's hushed sighs
laughter's vast vague foamy waves roll in.
But I
hang out in the reading room of the streets,
flipping the pages of the dictionary
whose words sound like eight-penny coffin nails hammered in.
Midnight's humid fingers
grab my prick,
a splintered fence looks like the enemy's teeth,
and the schizoid cathedral gallops
like hail on the dome's bald gold head.
I'll never know why I cruised this night
of unredeemed identity, of imagery
that can't describe the shape of my agony.
I've seen Christ extract himself from the nails on an icon —
first feet, then left hand, then right,
and the weeping mud kiss the hem of his gown.

Unfinished Poem | VLADIMIR MAYAKOVSKY

I pick off the petals and don't know
if she loves me, I rip off my own fingers
to find out, I pluck wayside daisies
to predict my fate, but nothing helps,

I shave or get a haircut
and see the gray everywhere,
I pray I'll still be free
to act, to be myself, and not to worry.

Our affair's over. The fragile rowboat
of love has smashed against the everyday.
We're finished. Let's not hurt each other
with accusations and regrets.

Look — how amazing the silence is!
Night praises the sky with stars.
In glorious hours like these
I want to speak to the years, to history, to the entire universe.

Words are so fierce they can kill you —
not the slick phrases you hear in the theatre-boxes
but words that open coffins, make the dead walk,
make coffins tremble on their four oak legs.

When I tighten my saddle I hear the hardware ring
for centuries, trains hiss and sidle in
to kiss poetry's hands. I know speech seems trivial,
petals crushed by a dancer's heel,

but the fact is — man, in his soul, his lips, his bones...

Attempt at Jealousy

| MARINA TSVETAYEVA

What's it like with another woman
simpler isn't it
one stroke of the oar
and I dissolved behind you
like a cloud like a coastline

What's it like with a nobody
no gift for poetry
in life in bed no gift
for the wild talk you love
what's it like to be with someone

trivial eat ordinary food keep busy
to feel your soul grow more and more alone
to look at her face and see a stranger
to want to sleep stricken by the still fresh
gash of immortal conscience

The Steel Cricket | INNOKENTY ANNENSKY

I knew anguish would come back and stay with me.
She tinkles and slams the watchmaker's lid
and whoever snaps it open for her
will screw the steel heart's quivering spring

to the chirp of wings, and unscrew it again.
The crickets beat their fiery wings impatiently.
Are they happy about the happiness that's possible?
Are they singing to end their pain?

They have so much to say and so far to go,
but our paths won't meet, little brothers!
Our friendship here is really a miracle.
We'll live together one more minute, that's all,

until the lid pops open, tinkles and slams,
then you'll be miles away where I can't hear you.
In a minute she'll come back on tiptoe and stay
with me — anguish — not you and your tender voices.

Bored Remembering | INNOKENTY ANNENSKY

Whenever I sit at my desk the same page dotted
and streaked with ink yawns at me.
I want to leave people but how
can I escape the night's misery.

Everybody has faded into the distance,
what never existed is clear.
Until dawn each line I forgot blurs
into a swollen black stain or a face.

One impossible answer: everything is me
where hallucinated letters burn in front of me...
I like children moving around in the house.
I like to hear them cry at night.

My Anxiety | INNOKENTY ANNENSKY

·Let the grass turn brown on top of my crazy skull.
Let my wax hand in the box disappear.
I'm convinced my confusion and pain
will continue to live in you, and my anxiety.

But not in those who love me and think I'm special
though I don't deserve their jealous, wild praise.
Ah the strength of people who love — gentle even in pain.
Their girlish tenderness heals invisibly.

Why should anyone be confused?
Love shines forever like the infinite depths of crystal.
But my love isn't love — it blows apart like a horse in the sky.
To her it's poison meat, something unreal.

Decorated with a wreath of withered azaleas,
love wants to sing but before the first line slips out
her children are captured and tied up.
Their hands have been broken. Their eyes are blind.

The Flame | INNOKENTY ANNENSKY

I thought my heart was empty and hard
like a stone,
I said it didn't matter if the fire's tongue
scorched it.

So I wasn't hurt at all,
or only a little,
but I know it's better if I
kill it while there's still time.

My heart's ripe with a darkness
like the grave's, the fire's out.
Now fumes from the black wick
choke me.

One Second | INNOKENTY ANNENSKY

The designs on your blouse are flickering so wildly,
the boiling dust is so white
we don't need smiles or words.
Stay like this,

almost invisible, sullen,
chalkier than the dusk in autumn
under this streaming willow.
The distance swells with shadow,

one second and the wind jumps past,
spilling the leaves,
one second and my heart wakes up
and feels that it isn't you.

Stay like this, not speaking
or smiling, a ghost.
Shadows meet, their edges quiver,
the dust listens. It's as soft as your hands.

August | INNOKENTY ANNENSKY

The clouds drift close to us,
the simmering red sun
softens to nothing through the haze.
Nothing but gloom comes from it.

The horses that pull the funeral cart
are silent, the coffin gleams,
the shield on the box flashes
and wanes as the sky catches in it.

It's late summer
among the willows, on the sand,
in front of the drained yellow flowers
of the shrinking wreath —

I thought the chrysanthemum
that nods like a human head
bent hopelessly
toward the coffin's polished lid

and the two twisted petals
on the tailboard of the hearse
were the gold circles
of the earrings she left behind.

Love | INNOKENTY ANNENSKY

I love the echo of iron wheels
that trails off into the woods,
I love a few minutes of boredom
after someone has laughed,

I love the purple half-light
that splashes over me on winter mornings,
the thin red glint of winter
instead of the hot spring sun.

I love colors dissolving into a haze of
shadow on the blurred horizon,
I love all the things in this world that don't
leave a trace or have anything else that's like them.

September | INNOKENTY ANNENSKY

The gardens are a dull gold,
the red wound of disease creeps everywhere,
the sun crawls and spills its heat
on the smelly fruit.

The rug is yellow silk, huge footprints are scattered on it.
We've swallowed the lie of our last meeting,
the stale fathomless pools in the parks
still wait for the peak of misery,

but the human heart sees only the beauty of what is lost,
the ecstasy of strength sucked in and killed.
Even people who've washed down their white pills
are excited by the cunty smells of autumn.

The Black Profile | INNOKENTY ANNENSKY

Right now I'm still alive
but we both hang on in the silence of growing fear,
we know we'll deceive each other without wanting to
and lie even to ourselves.

Now, looking in through the window, laced with frost,
the shadow of disease judges us
like one of those childhood angels we were told
guarded us at the headboard each night.

The ends of the circle of torment
lack only one link. I want to understand
that one moment, that fake paradise
when we held each other, but it's gone

into the pure light of morning before I can speak.
The landlord's garden is weedy and brown.
The door to it is forgotten,
snow's falling,

the black profile frozen into the
mirror of granite like a fossil
or the memory of someone's hand
touches my neck lovingly.

The Capital | INNOKENTY ANNENSKY

Winter. The city sleeps in its yellow mist.
Yellow snow rots on the pavements and bare ground.
I don't know where you are or where we are,
I just know we're together and can't be torn apart.

Were we invented by our leader's unshakable power?
Did the world forget to attack us until we sank?
We don't have any myths to look back on,
just stones and terrible facts,

things the magician gave us —
lies and a polluted river, the warm color of the fawn,
our own deserts, those numb squares
where citizens were hanged before dawn.

And whatever we had where we lived,
what launched our eagle, what chained
the giant who wore black laurels to the rock there —
all that will be happiness to our children.

He was so courageous, almost like a god!
His own violent horse of the unreal threw him.
Our dictator couldn't trample the snake of greed
so we worship it as the one God.

That's why we huddle together and call it love.
Our only peace is our children, we believe,
as we bend over their toys with them and feel safe
and hear the riderless beast of the state paw the roof.

Ballad Without Music

INNOKENTY ANNENSKY

The smoke of leaf fires thickens
but you can see through it.
Sometimes the wheelruts flare.
There's a cold drizzle.
We sit here, not quite touching.
Something keeps us from talking,
something shakes us.
No sound, not a remnant of melody
from the fields, from our own poor heads.
You snatch my cup
just before it touches my lips.

Poppies | INNOKENTY ANNENSKY

The day's on fire,
poppies everywhere —
impotent, hungry clumps,

lips swollen with lust and poison.
Red butterflies
stretch their wings, land

on the petals, but this garden's
choked with weeds
not lovers. Not a party

for years. The dry wrinkled blossoms
quiver like old ladies' heads
whose scalps burn under the white sky.

4 | *Sea Ice*

ESKIMO SONGS

Orpingalik's Song to
His Song-Brother

you I
remember you so well
song-brother
we were close
nobody beat us nobody outsang
our tongues
it was like this once
huge antlers
begin crossing the lake right there
ice glazes the kayak
our wives watch us from the bank
it was like this we're very young
the kayaks wait there all
bunched together like wolves
their long gray pointy noses
rest on the ice
let's chase it
on the big lake
you follow me can't
keep up fall back our wives
judging us as we run
I still see it brother

Orpingalik's Breath

I have to sing
a song about myself
sick since autumn
stretched out in bed
weak as a child

I'm so sad
I wish my woman
lived with another man
in the house of someone
who'd protect her a man
hard and strong as winter ice

once I could track down anything
white bear caribou seal I can still see
myself on foot beating the men in kayaks
the white bear threw me down but I stabbed it
the seal I thought got away I hooked it
now dawn after dawn rolls by
and I'm still sick
the lamp's cold

I'm so sad I
wish she'd go away
to a better man
so weak I can't even
get up out of bed

who knows what can happen to a man
I lie here drained unable to rise
remembering how I beat everyone
to this kill or that

and they all stood there
with nothing

no oil for the lamp
only my memories are strong

Igjugarjuk's Song

when I ran over the white spring fields
melting
I met the black musk ox
for the first time
its hair shining
grazing on flowers
on the hill where I stood
I was stupid to think
they were small and thin
I saw
when I got closer
they grew up out of the earth
giant shapes
far from our houses
black
in the fields of happy summer hunting
I wanted to shoot them
I crouched down
empty-handed

Akjartoq's Song

I take a deep breath
but it hurts it's too heavy
as I look for the song
the land fills with whispers
about my people starving
I don't know where

I look for the song
above me
and I forget how hard it was to breathe
remembering
when I could cut up and skin three huge beasts
cut them up
between the first and last hours
of the sun

Kivkarjuk's Song

I'm only a small woman
who likes to work
willing happy
I'll slave all day
at anything
I pluck willow buds
I love to go walking miles away
my soles worn through
and pluck willow buds
they feel silky like the wolf's chin

Sanik's Song

can't even get a good flame up
on my lamp
but I sing
my house my mistress trapped in darkness
I think about women
in my neighbors' houses
can't even keep a lamp burning right
not even a pale flicker

I just want everyone to feel happy

I remember
at so many places out there
I spotted a lovely seal
yes I remember between one place and another
in the water
a fat little seal
how I took him home
nobody else hunting there

as I came back toward home
my body felt so light

Mother's Song

it's quiet in the house so quiet
outside the snowstorm wails
the dogs curl up noses under their tails
my little son sleeps on his back
his mouth open
his belly rises and falls
breathing
is it strange if I cry for joy

The Boy Norqaut's Songs

you can bring down
a caribou
because you want to kill it
but this friend of mine
is like a lazy dog
he just lies there
when you track the white bear
and the black musk ox
over the ice
you have to work hard
to be as strong as they are

2

you can get strong
from being with people
who are strong
you stand there looking at
their teeth
when they smile
you smile better and have big
white teeth like theirs

Omatoq's Song

I wanted to take
everybody's woman
and they swam past me there
inside my head
outside
at the ice hole
the one with dark hair on her face
and the others
yes me
the one without children
a poor dog nothing else
so I wanted to take
everybody's woman
but all I found was the trail
of a spindly calf
I saw it crept up behind it
it wasn't afraid
me lonely yes without anyone
except that little one

Orpingalik's Wife Sings about Their Son

I
find
part of a song again
and it's a human thing it's human

why
should I be ashamed
of the child I carried inside
just because he killed someone and ran away

if I'm ashamed
it's because I'm not
perfect as the blue sky or as
wise

now what others say about him will teach him
how bad he is
and I'm ashamed because he's mine
because he can't help me when I'm old

I envy everyone with all their
friends waving behind them as they
leave for home after a feast
what happiness!

I remember that winter
when we left the island the air was warm
the melting snow sang under the runners
I was so beautiful so tame

but when I heard about the killing
about my son running away the earth
turned into a mountain its peak was a needle
I stood wherever I was trembling

Uvavnuk's Song

the sea the huge sea's making me move like this
cut off from land
moving me like the weed moves in a river

the arch of the sky the great force of storms
moving the spirit in me
until I'm carried away

a grassblade shaken and torn with joy

Morning Song of the Wizard Aua

I get up to meet the day
I break from my sleep
quick as the crow's wing

I gaze toward dawn
my face turns away from the darkness
toward the dawn whitening

Spirit Song

are my feet big enough
are they big
my huge feet
are my indoor shoes big enough
my huge indoor shoes
and what about my gigantic thighs
that hold me up
O the things that hold me up
are so big
my body's huge
my back's powerful
my head's enormous
O the things that hold me up

Bad Weather Hunting Song

not even the words I put together balanced perfectly on
     the tip of my tongue
broke up the clouds heavy with sleet over the sea
I stood in my boat on land I saw the sky turn gray
it felt like a turd was in my mouth to have my best
     hunting song ready
useless

A Poor Man's Prayer
to the Spirits

fatherless ones
motherless ones
give me skin boots
give me
one of those beasts
that make delicious blood soup
the biggest
not from the earth
from the bottom of the sea

you ones without father
or mother Oh
bring me a gift

Spirit Song

I walked on the ice of the sea
seals blowing at the holes
and I was amazed when I heard
the voice of the sea
and the creepy sighing of the ice
that had just formed
I looked behind men and women
deep into what's hidden
smoothing wrinkles
my boot-thong loose
I could hear the voice say
keep going

Wearing the Skin of the Great Northern Diver

I'm stretching out my arms wide
thank you thank you
because food came to me
I feel so good
here's why
I was hiding waiting
for a caribou bull
it came
its long tangled antlers up
its flank facing me
what a hiding place I have I
didn't even look I
just shot right through its shoulders
it sank crumpled onto
the bare earth
pissing all the way!
I feel so good
here's why
a big dog-seal
blew through its breathing hole
and I a
man
stood right up there
and grew became a huge tall man
and hooked its neck
with my harpoon

Avane's Song

just because I hunt and find nothing
am I old and worthless
I used to stand straight and shoot
my arrows flew out so fast
I didn't have time to aim
the bulls fell
I hit them
their wide arching horns looked beautiful
Oh I can't stop looking
in the hills
I can't wait to find them
I saw those huge horns crash to the ground
I saw their muzzles sink deep into the mud

A Song from the Time of Waiting for Something to Break

autumn breaks in blowing
I shiver as the raw wind
hits me
it doesn't care if I die
the waves beat my kayak so hard
I almost capsize
and I shiver terrified
of the ooze at the bottom of the water
I almost never see calm water
the waves push me everywhere
I shake when I think about
how the gulls will hack at my dead body

Spirit Song

spirit in the sky
come down here
right away
bite the world to death

I rise
up to the spirits
magician friends help me
reach the spirits

child child child
spirit
that can bite evil
come to us

and spirit at the bottom of the
earth I'm calling you I
live near you on top
bite our enemies

join your brother from the sky
each bite an eye out
of evil's face
so it can't see us

An Old Song of the Sun, the Moon, and the Fear of Loneliness

sitting with friends
I'm afraid
when I feel myself wanting
to be alone
and afraid
being alone

it's beautiful
when summer comes to the world
there's such joy watching
the sun
follow its ancient road

Oh I'm afraid
when winter comes to the world
and I watch the half-moon
and the full moon
follow their ancient roads

I let out what my heart
is crying
but only I hear it
where is everything going
I wish I were east a thousand miles

but whatever happens whatever
I think I'll never meet
those people
with the same blood
as mine again

Dead Man's Song Dreamed
by Someone Alive

I'm so happy
when it's dawn
when the sun crawls
up over the sky

without this
I'd be scared I couldn't eat
I'd see maggots
eat their way in
at the bottom of my collarbone
and in my eyes

here I am remembering
how choked with fear I was
when they buried me
in a snow hut out on the lake
when the last block of snow
was pushed in I couldn't see
how my soul would fly
to the land of hunting

the doorblock worried me
I shit
when the freshwater ice split in the cold
and the frost crack grew
thundering up over the sky

life was a glory
in winter
but did it make me happy?

no! I was always anxious
to get sealskins and kamik skins

I'm so happy now
every time dawn
stains the night sky white
every time the sun rolls up
over the heavens

Anonymous

maybe it doesn't matter but
what about him
he sat there boiling
in the middle of all the women
eyes furious bent like a horn
ready to be cut into spears
alone
well I'm just singing about this man who couldn't
     do anything
blame my tongue it puts words
together
blame my mouth that moves
that curls down at the corners
a bent twig
ready to be used for a kayak rib

Kanaihuaq's Attack on Utahania

I'm here but
how can I be singing this
I have to
I was told
when spring came
you and your uncle's sister
crept out together alone
and fucked
you just hid out and fucked
did she spread her legs nice and wide
come on tell me
was she hard right above where
you stuck it into her
I know I'm not much good at
singing maybe this is
too long but
I don't lie everybody
says it
you two went out
and fucked until you
couldn't stand up

Utahania's Attack on Kanaihuaq

you you
think you know everything
because white men
listen to you
why should they
so you
drove to see
the East-people
so you figured out how to
write down the things we say
with A B C
so what
your hand's a machine
you think that's what a chief is
that's wisdom
asshole!
this is
me
singing just to be mean
just to make you feel like shit
the way a bird does
when it's hungry by screeching
its beak against trees stones ice
and gets no food

Anonymous

who is it is it death
who is it is
death going to throw its house over me
get off
or I'll hitch my dogs to your head and
they'll tear it off

An Old Man Cries Out
into the Driving Snow

cold and mosquitoes
never come together
crappy pests
I lie on the ice
on the snowy ice
and listen to my teeth sing
their dumb chattering song
and know
this is me really me
me

Tuglik's Song

put on all the bracelets beads rings
we own for this
we're only girls
huddled together
in hard times without food
bellies shrunken
dishes empty
but suddenly
we feel lovely
our skin boats float through the air
the ropes fly too
the earth's
loose in the air
look way out there
see it
the men drag beautiful seals home
there's plenty again
remember
the smell of the bubbling pots
slabs of blubber slapped down by the side bench
feast days keep us together
hug them kiss them
they bring us so much

Shaman Song

I remember when
my spirit helper
got weak I
worried about the secrets
now I feel small
I'm afraid of what men
think about me
now
calling my helper back is
like afterbirth
stuck in my throat
I can't breathe
I can see the sky
and I move like heavy ice
on top of the ocean
muscles tight
teeth clenched
filled with joy
now my helper and I
kill the evils
my arms bloody
my jacket torn
back in the hut
the first time my spirit came to me
my teeth shivering
I was all I could say

Shaman Ahgutingmarik's
Magic Song

what moves what
moves me
somewhere out over the earth far from here
moves and is seen
has no bowels
wants to do bad things
comes right at us
O spirit
everybody's afraid
we wait in this hut
be here help me
say something
everybody's here inside
everybody whispers
I look up to the sky
eyes shut
hands together
coughing each word
I go out with my friend
into the cold black night
all night
the evils
now
back inside the lamps are out
keep your eyes shut

Shaman Ahgutingmarik's
Magic Song

earth everywhere earth
everywhere on earth
bones
bleached by the gods
sun air
flesh melts
O spirit
pour into my arms and legs
but don't dry them
don't turn them into bones
make me strong standing here
over the crow I shot down
flapping at my feet
screaming in fear while I
say whatever comes

Magic Words to Stop Bleeding

this blood
is from the baby sparrow's mother
wipe it off your cheek
this blood
came from wood
wipe it off

Magic Words to Cure a Sick Child

O my tiny child
my breasts are dripping with milk
for you
open your mouth and suck
drink
climb the mountain
up at the top you'll be healthy
you'll live a long long time

Unaleq's Song of the Beginning

everything broke
then rain
then the earth broke
two men sprang up from chunks of earth
soon one was the mother
then the father sang
O I'm a human being
here
I have a penis
here
let the hole at its tip be very wide
very very wide
I want it to open open open
because my baby's coming through it right
now

Last Song

how
can I walk on that thing
down there
the gigantic new sea ice
it croons like a mother to her young
anxiously it
sings through the whole land
listen
it's the one down there the
enormous sea ice beginning
crooning like a mother
singing to us everywhere
but listen
a man
it's true yes
I
a man
actually gaze at it I can
see it
it follows me and
this is true really
it thinks about me!

Appendix

ON "FIRST SONG / BANKEI: 1653"

Peter Haskell's translation of Bankei's "Song of Original Mind (Honshin no uta)," published in his *Bankei Zen*, Grove Press, 1984, formed the basis of "First Song." I read his version again and again —then—tired, irritable, and helpless from listening to my mother ramble in the aftermath of a serious year-long illness, for the greed of my baffled ear, one day I found myself beginning this vastly different poem. Much later, the last three stanzas came, inspired by other Bankei pieces from the same wonderful book.

ON "DAITO'S MIND"

Ken Kraft asked me to help him with translations of Daito, some of which appear in his book *Eloquent Zen*. My poem, "Daito's Mind," takes several of Daito's poems, based on Ken's translations, twisted into versions with lines of my own that form one running meditation. The last four lines are Daito's "death poem."

ON BUSON'S "ONE FIREFLY"

I've always felt the three-line haiku is impossible to bring off in English. When I came across Sawa and Shiffert's *Haiku Master Buson* and saw so many haiku by the man who painted the overwhelming *Rock Screen,* (the basis of a poem, "The Rocks," in my book *In It*), I wanted to find another way of re-creating some of them. After working with a selection from their book, keeping the three-line form, I decided to compress each poem into single lines (strange to skim the book again now, and see the Japanese printed one line straight across) making it a serial poem — Buson's "One Firefly" — whose rough theme is Buson's wandering toward death. In a letter, he says, "There are no gateways to Haikai. There is only the Hakiai gateway itself....A gateway exists naturally....Think for yourself about what you have inside yourself. There is no other way....It is best if you acquire haiku naturally."

Haiku perception, that brief abrupt glimpse of...?, is rare in English poetry. From her marvelous book, *Metaphysics as a Guide to Morals*, here is Iris Murdoch on haiku: "The Japanese haiku is a very short poem with a strict formal structure, which points, sometimes in a paradoxical way, at some aspect of the physical world. It indicates that the other does not lose or subjectivize the world. Zen painting also combines a skill, born of long and strict teaching, with a throwaway simplicity. In a few strokes, the pointless presence, the thereness of the plant, the animal, the man." Or, as Simone Weil puts it, "Attention: without thinking about." For me, the traditional three-line model, grafted onto English, cannot enact this vision of ...let's call it, for now, "the impossibility of paradigm."[1]

ON "NOTHING IN THE WORD / AZTEC SONGS"

The most humane quality of these poems, so perhaps the most memorable, is that they state directly (and with a touch of hysteria) man's primary experience of his relationship with God or the gods: unknowable, helplessly stupid, prayerful, necessary, but out of reach except in terms of speech that expresses a need for this primary relationship.

A man can say anything he wants "to God," for whatever reasons, but if he will not confess that this attempted dialogue with its

---

[1] From *Empire of Signs*, Roland Barthes, pp 69–84, the most interesting commentary on haiku I've ever read. Hill and Wang, 1982, translated by Richard Howard.

eternally missing reply is absurdity and despair I would rather not trust him. One has to decide whether the humiliation, the childishly begging tone, has advantages over certain dazzling (although I believe self-deceptive) intellectual positions. Those positions can be chosen for the brilliance of their insight, for how radically they upset other positions; but there are other ways of presenting the one-sided dialogue which seems to continue at the core of human life, whatever attraction this or that intellectual strategy may have.

I believe there is a voice with no skin on it in all of us. It is not a wonderfully complicated thoughtful voice. But it is the first way we respond to tragedy before our defenses begin to think us back to a calmer level of existence, to understanding. Meanwhile, it does happen that losses occur that reach into us and call out voices that may be directed at the sky. "Origin is the goal" and "In our greatest need we can only address the Unknown." Some way through all this may allow men to praise. I think these poems express that possibility too.

ON FINDING AND TRANSLATING RADNÓTI TOGETHER

One night at Frank's Bar in Philadelphia, we were sitting and drinking, talking about war. Weeks back, we had asked Steve Polgar to bring some translations of Hungarian poetry for us to read. I had joked about my Hungarian ancestry, about the nuttiness of Hungarians I had met, about my father's way of being Hungarian. Always the sting of death in any pleasure, always the sadness of parting and the fear of injury.

That night Polgar arrived at the bar with a few anthologies and we started reading. The translations were incredibly dead English. But when we stumbled on the Radnóti, Jeff Marks felt something very human and original drifting up through the mist of the translations. We began meeting regularly to "do justice" to poems we felt had been buried by the versions we saw, poems we felt were beautifully strong and poems we began to realize had been written under conditions where either silence or madness should have been the only alternatives left to a human being. We sat for hours, working with dictionaries, with the first bare English versions Polgar made, with our responses and suggestions, reading the successive versions back to each other, arguing over this line, that liberty, and this equivalent. One of us typed constantly to record what we did. There were moments of inspiration when almost an entire poem suddenly broke through all the silence between languages. Polgar thinks we have come unusually close to re-creating Radnóti's tone and political vision. I can't say. I tried to keep myself between two languages, one of which was practically nonsense to me, one of which can slip away and become, though still familiar, merely ordinary.

But between them is another language. I mean that during the process of struggling for the English version of a poem you want to re-create and make exciting reading, there is no language exactly, only broken webs, shadow accuracies, error enraged and impatient —you become anonymous and then leap out into a new attempt. You keep remembering Radnóti's enslavement by the Nazis in labor camps, in an extermination camp, and finally his death by shooting at the hands of an SS man. You remember most of all your own silences faced with the brutalities of governments and of men, and you are drawn back to men, whatever they may be, by the calm innocent heroism of speech in Miklós Radnóti's poems. You realize that there is no technique for bringing back the dead.

ON "HEAR THE MOTHER / TLINGIT SONGS"
I based my versions of Tlingit songs on transcriptions deposited in the University of Pennsylvania Anthropology Museum Library.

ON "SEA ICE / ESKIMO SONGS"
On the library shelves of The University of Pennsylvania Museum of Anthropology, I came across the Eskimo songs collected and transliterated by Knud Rasmussen in his ten-volume *Report of the Fifth Thule Expedition,* 1921–24. Those simple, unformed utterances opened me to a new mind, and I was impelled to rewrite several of them. They became *Sea Ice.* As I remember, Rasmussen also provided commentaries that helped to orient my sense of the poems

within their strange culture. I felt a bit hesitant about raiding some of the lyric salvage of his heroic expedition, but if I have made what he brought back more accessible to common readers, then I hope that balances things out. It seemed to be a kind of exoneration when my manuscript was awarded the Columbia University Translation Center Prize.

My temperament and wavering esthetic theories had me re-create these poems somewhere between Rasmussen's literalism and my own commitment to free invention. His texts, I think, were done almost as prose — lines separated by slashes running across the page. The shapes my versions took, I wish to believe, issue from imagining the unimaginable: how could a Philadelphia Jew, reading a Greenlander-Danish explorer's transcriptions of Eskimo poetry delivered vocally in the field, even graze cultural authenticity? What are these then?

Index

255

ABOUT THE AUTHOR

Stephen Berg is the author of *New & Selected Poems, Crow with No Mouth: Ikkyū, Oblivion, With Akhmatova at the Black Gates,* and many other books of poetry. He is cotranslator, with Diskin Clay, of Sophocles's *Oedipus the King,* and with Steven Polgar and S.J. Marks, of *Clouded Sky* by Miklós Radnóti. The recipient of Guggenheim, NEA, Dietrich Foundation, and Pew Foundation fellowships, he is founder and coeditor of the *American Poetry Review.* He and painter Thomas Chimes were commissioned by the Fairmount Park Art Association to create the public art project "Sleeping Woman," installed in 1991 along Philadelphia's Kelly Drive on the edge of the Schuylkill River. He is currently Professor of Humanities at the University of the Arts in Philadelphia.

COLOPHON

This book was designed and composed in the typeface Bembo by Scribe Typography, Port Townsend, Washington. Like many of the poems in this book, this typeface is a version. In 1929 Monotype attempted to capture the spirit of type engraved on steel punches and cast in metal during the 15th century. The name "Bembo" refers to the book that inspired them, a travelogue about Mt. Aetna written by Pietro Bembo in 1495 set in type designed by Francesco Griffo. Griffo's lively refinements to the roman letter are with us today in many highly readable faces. The printing is by Malloy Lithographing, Inc. on Glatfelter Author's, an acid-free, 85% recycled (10% post-consumer) stock.